MATURITY

ALSO BY OSHO

MATURITY

The Responsibility
of Being Oneself

osho

·

insights for a
new way of living

St. Martin's Griffin ❧ New York

MATURITY: THE RESPONSIBILITY OF BEING ONESELF. Copyright ©
1999 by Osho International Foundation. All rights reserved. Printed
in the United States of America. No part of this book may be used or
reproduced in any manner whatsoever without written permission
except in the case of brief quotations embodied in critical articles or
reviews. For information address St. Martin's Press, 175 Fifth Avenue,
New York, N.Y. 10010.

Book design by Claire Vaccaro

Library of Congress Cataloging-in-Publication Data

Osho, 1931–1990.
    Maturity : the responsibility of being oneself / Osho. — 1st St. Martin's Griffin ed.
       p.   cm. — (Insights for a new way of living)
    ISBN 0-312-20561-9
    1. Spiritual life. 2. Self-realization—Religious aspects. 3. Maturation
(Psychology)—Religious aspects.   I. Title.
BP605.R43 M38 1999
299'.93 21—dc21   99-032893

First Edition: November 1999

1   3   5   7   9   10   8   6   4   2

Contents

✧

Contents

Foreword

ᘒ

The Art of Living

Man is born to achieve life, but it all depends on him. He can miss it. He can go on breathing, he can go on eating, he can go on growing old, he can go on moving toward the grave—but this is not life, this is gradual death. From the cradle to the grave . . . a seventy-year-long gradual death. And because millions of people around you are dying in this gradual, slow death, you also start imitating them. Children learn everything from those who are around them, and we are surrounded by the dead.

So first we have to understand what I mean by "life." It must not be simply growing old, it must be growing up. And these are two different things.

Growing old, any animal is capable of. Growing up is the prerogative of human beings.

Only a few claim the right.

Growing up means moving every moment deeper into the principle of life; it means going farther away from death—not toward death. The deeper you go into life, the more you understand the immortality within you. You are going away from death; a moment comes when you can see that death is nothing but changing clothes, or changing houses, changing forms—nothing dies, nothing *can* die.

Death is the greatest illusion there is.

For growing up, just watch a tree. As the tree grows up its roots are growing down, deeper. There is a balance—the higher the tree goes the deeper the roots will go. You cannot have a tree one hundred and fifty feet high with small roots; they could not support such a huge tree.

> Maturity means the same as innocence, only with one difference: it is innocence reclaimed, it is innocence recaptured.

In life, growing up means growing deep within yourself—that's where your roots are.

To me, the first principle of life is meditation. Everything else comes second. And childhood is the best time. As you grow older it means you are coming closer to death, and it becomes more and more difficult to go into meditation.

Meditation means going into your immortality, going into your eternity, going into your godliness. And the child is the most qualified person because he is still unburdened by knowledge, unburdened by religion, unburdened by education, unburdened by all kinds of rubbish. He is innocent.

But unfortunately his innocence is condemned as ignorance. Ignorance and innocence have a similarity, but they are not the same. Ignorance is also a state of not knowing, just as innocence is—but there is a great difference too, which has been overlooked

by the whole of humanity up to now. Innocence is not knowledgeable, but it is not desirous of being knowledgeable either. It is
utterly content, fulfilled.

A small child has no ambitions, he has no desires. He is so
absorbed in the moment—a bird on the wing catches his eye so
totally; a butterfly, its beautiful colors, and he is enchanted; the
rainbow in the sky . . . and he cannot
conceive that there can be anything
more significant, richer than this
rainbow. And the night full of stars,
stars beyond stars . . .

Innocence is rich, it is full, it is
pure.

Ignorance is poor, it is a beggar—
it wants this, it wants that, it wants to
be knowledgeable, it wants to be re-
spectable, it wants to be wealthy, it
wants to be powerful. Ignorance
moves on the path of desire. Innocence is a state of desirelessness.
But because both are without knowledge, we have remained confused
about their natures. We have taken it
for granted that they are the same.

The first step in the art of living

> Maturity is a rebirth, a spiritual birth. You are born anew, you are a child again. With fresh eyes you start looking at existence. With love in the heart you approach life. With silence and innocence you penetrate your own innermost core.

will be to understand the distinction between ignorance and innocence. Innocence has to be supported, protected—because the
child has brought with him the greatest treasure, the treasure that
sages find only after arduous effort. Sages have said that they become

children again, that they are reborn. In India the real Brahman, the real knower, has called himself *dwij*, twice born. Why twice born? What happened to the first birth? What is the need of the second birth? And what is he going to gain in the second birth?

In the second birth he is going to gain what was available in the first birth, but the society, the parents, the people surrounding him crushed it, destroyed it. Every child is being stuffed with knowledge. His simplicity has to be somehow removed, because simplicity is not going to help him in this competitive world. His simplicity will look to the world as if he is a simpleton; his innocence will be exploited in every possible way. Afraid of the society, afraid of the world we ourselves have created, we try to make every child be clever, cunning, knowledgeable—to be in the category of the powerful, not in the category of the oppressed and the powerless.

And once the child starts growing in the wrong direction, he goes on moving that way—his whole life moves in that direction. Whenever you understand that you have missed life, the first principle to be brought back is innocence. Drop your knowledge, forget your scriptures, forget your religions, your theologies, your philosophies. Be born again, become innocent—and it is in your hands. Clean your mind of all that is not known by you, of all that is borrowed, all that has come from tradition, convention. All that has been given to you by others—parents, teachers, universities— just get rid of it. Once again be simple, once again be a child. And this miracle is possible by meditation.

Meditation is simply a strange surgical method that cuts you away from all that is not yours and saves only that which is your authentic being. It burns everything else and leaves you standing naked, alone under the sun, in the wind. It is as if you are the first man who has descended onto earth—who knows nothing, who has to discover everything, who has to be a seeker, who has to go on a pilgrimage.

The second principle is the pilgrimage. Life must be a seeking—not a desire but a search; not an ambition to become this, to become that, a president of a country or prime minister of a country, but a search to find out "Who am I?"

It is very strange that people who don't know who they are, are trying to become somebody. They don't even know who they are right now! They are unacquainted with their being—but they have a goal of becoming.

Becoming is the disease of the soul.

Being is you.

And to discover your being is the beginning of life. Then each moment is a new discovery, each moment

> Growing old, any animal is capable of. Growing up is the prerogative of human beings. Only a few claim the right.

brings a new joy. A new mystery opens its doors, a new love starts growing in you, a new compassion that you have never felt before, a new sensitivity about beauty, about goodness. You become so sensitive that even the smallest blade of grass takes on an immense importance for you. Your sensitivity makes it clear to you that this small blade of grass is as important to existence as the biggest star; without this blade of grass, existence would be less than it is. This small blade of grass is unique, it is irreplaceable, it has its own individuality.

And this sensitivity will create new friendships for you—friend-ships with trees, with birds, with animals, with mountains, with rivers, with oceans, with stars. Life becomes richer as love grows, as friendliness grows.

In the life of St. Francis there is a beautiful incident. He is dying, and he has always traveled on a donkey from place to place sharing his experiences. All his disciples are gathered to listen to his last words. The last words of a man are always the most significant that he has ever uttered because they contain the whole experience of his life.

But what the disciples heard, they could not believe. . . .

St. Francis did not address the disciples, he addressed the donkey. He said, "Brother, I am immensely indebted to you. You have been carrying me from one place to another place with never a complaint, never grumbling. Before I leave this world, all that I want is forgiveness from you; I have not been humane to you." These were the last words of St. Francis. A tremendous sensitivity to say to the donkey, "Brother donkey . . . ," and asking to be forgiven.

As you become more sensitive, life becomes bigger. It is not a small pond; it becomes oceanic. It is not confined to you and your wife and your children—it is not confined at all. This whole ex-istence becomes your family, and unless the whole existence is your family you have not known what life is—because no man is an island, we are all connected.

We are a vast continent, joined in millions of ways.

And if our hearts are not full of love for the whole, in the same proportion our life is cut short.

Meditation will bring you sensitivity, a great sense of belonging to the world. It is our world—the stars are ours, and we are not foreigners here. We belong intrinsically to existence. We are part of it, we are *heart* of it.

Second, meditation will bring you a great silence—because all rubbish knowledge is gone. Thoughts that are part of the knowledge are gone too . . . an immense silence, and you are surprised: this silence is the only music there is.

All music is an effort to bring this silence somehow into manifestation. The seers of the ancient East have been very emphatic about the point that all the great arts—music, poetry, dance, painting, sculpture—all are born out of meditation. These arts are an effort to in some way bring the unknowable into the world of the known for those who are not ready for the pilgrimage—they are gifts for those who are not ready to go on the pilgrimage. Perhaps a song may trigger a desire to go in search of the source, perhaps a statue.

> Life must be a seeking—not a desire but a search; not an ambition to become this, to become that, a president of a country or prime minister of a country, but a search to find out "Who am I?"

The next time you enter a temple of Gautam Buddha, just sit silently, watch the statue. Because the statue has been made in such a way, in such proportions that if you watch it you will fall silent. It is a statue of meditation; it is not concerned with Gautam Buddha.

That's why all those statues look alike—Mahavira, Gautam Buddha, Neminatha, Adinatha. . . . The twenty-four tirthankaras of the Jainas . . . in the same temple you will find twenty-four statues all alike, exactly alike. In my childhood I used to ask my father, "Can you explain to me how it is possible that twenty-four persons are exactly alike—the same size, the same nose, the same face, the same body . . . ?"

And he used to say, "I don't know. I am always puzzled myself that there is not a bit of difference. And it is almost unheard of—there are not even two persons in the whole world who are alike, what to say about twenty-four?"

But as my meditation blossomed I found the answer—not from anybody else, I found the answer that these statues have nothing to do with the people. These statues have something to do with what was happening inside those twenty-four people, and that happening was exactly the same. We have not bothered about the outside; we have insisted that only the inner should be paid attention to. The outer is unimportant. Somebody is young, somebody is old, somebody is black, somebody is white, somebody is man, somebody is woman—it does not matter; what matters is that inside there is an ocean of silence. In that oceanic state, the body takes a certain posture.

You have observed it yourself, but you have not been alert. When you are angry, have you observed? Your body takes a certain posture. In anger you cannot keep your hands open; in anger—the fist. In anger you cannot smile—or can you? With a certain emotion, the body has to follow a certain posture.

So those statues are made in such a way that if you simply sit silently and watch, and then close your eyes, a negative, shadow image enters into your body and you start feeling something you have not felt before. Those statues and temples were not built for worshiping; they were built for experiencing. They are scientific laboratories—they have nothing to do with religion! A certain secret science has been used for centuries so the coming generations could come in contact with the experiences of the older generations. Not through books, not through words, but through something that goes deeper—through silence, through meditation, through peace.

As your silence grows, your friendliness, your love grows; your life becomes a moment-to-moment dance, a joy, a celebration.

Have you ever thought about why, all over the world, in every culture, in every society, there are a few days in the year for celebration? These few days for celebration are just a compensation—because these societies have taken away all the celebration of your life, and if nothing is given to you in compensation your life can become a danger to the culture.

Every culture has to give some compensation to you so that you don't feel completely lost in misery, in sadness. But these compensations are false.

Firecrackers and colored lights cannot make you rejoice. They are only for children—for you they are just a nuisance. But in your inner world there can be a continuity of lights, songs, joys.

Always remember that society compensates you when it feels that the repressed may explode into a dangerous situation if it is not compensated. The society finds some way of allowing you to let out the repressed—but this is not true celebration, and it cannot be true.

True celebration should come from your life, in your life.

And true celebration cannot be according to the calendar, that on the first of November you will celebrate. Strange, the whole year you are miserable and on the first of November suddenly you come out of misery, dancing? Either the misery was false or the first of November is false; both cannot be true. And once the first of November is gone you are back in your dark hole, everybody in his misery, everybody in his anxiety.

Life should be a continuous celebration, a festival of lights the whole year round. Only then can you grow up, can you blossom.

Transform small things into celebration.

For example, in Japan they have the tea ceremony. In every Zen monastery and in every person's house who can afford it they have a small temple for drinking tea. Now, tea is no longer an ordinary, profane thing; they have transformed it into a celebration. The temple for drinking tea is made in a certain way—in a beautiful garden, with a beautiful pond, swans in the pond, flowers all around. Guests come and they have to leave their shoes outside; it is a temple. And as you enter the temple you cannot speak; you have to leave your thinking and thoughts and speech outside with your shoes. You sit down in a meditative posture and the host, the woman who prepares tea for you—her movements are so graceful, as if she is dancing, moving around preparing tea, putting cups and saucers before you as if you are gods. With such respect . . . she will bow down, and you will receive it with the same respect.

The tea is prepared in a special samovar, which makes beautiful sounds, a music of its own. And it is part of the tea ceremony that everybody should listen first to the music of the tea. So everybody is silent, listening . . . birds chirping outside in the garden, and the samovar . . . the tea is creating its own song. A peace surrounds. . . .

When the tea is ready and it is poured into everybody's cup, you are not just to drink it the way people are doing everywhere. First you will smell the aroma of the tea. You will sip the tea as if it has come from the beyond, you will take time—there is no hurry. Somebody may start playing on the flute or on the sitar. An ordinary thing—just tea—and they have made it a beautiful religious festival. Everybody comes out of it nourished, fresh, feeling younger, feeling juicier.

And what can be done with tea can be done with everything— with your clothes, with your food. People are living almost in sleep; otherwise every fabric, every cloth has its own beauty, its own feel. If you are sensitive, then the clothing is not just to cover your body, then it is something expressing your individuality, something expressing your taste, your culture, your being. Everything you do should be expressive of you; it should have your signature on it. Then life becomes a continuous celebration.

Even if you fall sick and you are lying in bed, you will make those moments of lying in bed moments of beauty and joy, moments of relaxation and rest, moments of meditation, moments of listening to music or to poetry. There is no need to be sad that you are sick. You should be happy that everybody is in the office and you are in your bed like a king, relaxing—somebody is preparing tea for you, the samovar is singing a song, a friend has offered to come and play flute for you. . . .

These things are more important than any medicine. When you are sick, call a doctor. But more important, call those who love you because there is no medicine more important than love. Call those who can create beauty, music, poetry around you because there is nothing that heals like a mood of celebration. Medicine is the lowest kind of treatment—but it seems we have forgotten everything, so we have to depend on medicine and be grumpy and sad, as if you are missing some great joy that you were having in the office! In the office you were miserable—just one day off and you cling to misery, too—you won't let it go.

Make everything creative, make the best out of the worst—that's what I call the art of living. And if a man has lived his whole life making every moment and every phase of it a beauty, a love, a joy, naturally his death is going to be the ultimate peak of his whole life's endeavor. The last touches . . . his death is not going to be ugly as it ordinarily happens every day to everyone.

If death is ugly, that means your whole life has been a waste. Death should be a peaceful acceptance, a loving entry into the unknown, a joyful good-bye to old friends, to the old world. There should not be any tragedy in it.

One Zen Master, Lin Chi, was dying. Thousands of his disciples had gathered to listen to the last sermon, but Lin Chi was simply lying down—joyous, smiling, but not saying a single word.

Seeing that he was going to die and he was not saying a single word, somebody reminded Lin Chi—an old friend, a Master in his own right; he was not a disciple of Lin Chi, that's why he could say to him—"Lin Chi, have you forgotten that you have to say your last words? I have always said your memory isn't right. You are dying . . . have you forgotten?"

Lin Chi said, "Just listen." And on the roof two squirrels were running, screeching. And he said, "How beautiful," and he died.

For a moment, when he said "Just listen," there was absolute silence. Everybody thought he was going to say something great, but only two squirrels fighting, screeching, running on the roof. . . . And he smiled and he died. But he has given his last message: don't make things small and big, trivial and important. Everything is important. At this moment, Lin Chi's death is as important as the two squirrels running on the roof, there is no difference. In existence it is all the same. That was his whole philosophy, his whole life's teaching—that there is nothing that is great and there is nothing that is small; it all depends on you, what you make out of it.

Start with meditation, and things will go on growing in you—silence, serenity, blissfulness, sensitivity. And whatever comes out of meditation, try to bring it out in life. Share it, because everything shared grows fast. And when you have reached the point of death, you will know there is no death. You can say good-bye, there is no need for any tears of sadness—maybe tears of joy, but not of sadness.

But you have to begin from being innocent.

So first, throw out all crap that you are carrying—and everybody is carrying so much crap! One wonders, for what? Just because people have been telling you that these are great ideas, principles . . . You have not been intelligent with yourself. Be intelligent with yourself.

Life is very simple, it is a joyful dance. And the whole earth can be full of joy and dance, but there are people who are seriously vested in their interest that nobody should enjoy life, that nobody should smile, that nobody should laugh, that life is a sin, that it is a punishment. How can you enjoy life when the climate is such that you have been told continually that it is a punishment, that you are suffering because you have done wrong things, and it is a kind of jail where you have been thrown to suffer?

I say to you life is not a jail, it is not a punishment. It is a reward, and it is given only to those who have earned it, who deserve it. Now it is your right to enjoy; it will be a sin if you *don't* enjoy. It will be against existence if you don't beautify it, if you leave it just as you have found it. No, leave it a little happier, a little more beautiful, a little more fragrant.

Listen to your being. It is continuously giving you hints; it is a still, small voice. It does not shout at you, that is true. And if you are a little silent you will start feeling your way. Be the person you are. Never try to be another, and you will become mature. *Maturity is accepting the responsibility of being oneself,* whatsoever the cost. *Risking all to be oneself,* that's what maturity is all about.

DEFINITIONS

❧

FROM IGNORANCE TO INNOCENCE

Maturity means the same as innocence, only with one difference: it is innocence reclaimed, it is innocence recaptured. Every child is born innocent, but every society corrupts him. Every society, up to now, has been a corruptive influence on every child. All cultures have depended on exploiting the innocence of the child, on exploiting the child, on making him a slave, on conditioning him for their own purposes, for their own ends—political, social, ideological. Their whole effort has been how to recruit the child as a slave for some purpose. Those purposes are decided by the vested interests. The priests and the politicians have been in a deep conspiracy, they have been working together.

The moment the child starts becoming part of your society he starts losing something immensely valuable; he starts losing contact with God. He becomes more and more hung up in the head, he forgets all about the heart—and the heart is the bridge that leads to being. Without the heart you cannot reach your own being—it is impossible. From the head there is no way directly to being; you have to go via the heart, and all societies are destructive to the heart. They are against love, they are against feelings; they condemn feelings as sentimentality. They condemned all lovers down the ages for the simple reason that love is not of the head, it is of the heart. A man who is capable of love is sooner or later going to discover his being—and once a person discovers his being he is free from all structures, from all patterns. He is free from all bondage. He is pure freedom.

Every child is born innocent, but every child is made knowledgeable by the society. Hence schools, colleges, universities exist; their function is to destroy you, to corrupt you.

> ᶌ
>
> From the head there is no way directly to being; you have to go via the heart—and all societies are destructive to the heart.

Maturity means gaining your lost innocence again, reclaiming your paradise, becoming a child again. Of course it has a difference—the ordinary child is bound to be corrupted, but when you reclaim your childhood you become incorruptible. Nobody can corrupt you, you become intelligent enough—now you know what the society has done to you and you are alert and aware, you will not allow it to happen again.

Maturity is a rebirth, a spiritual birth. You are born anew, you are a child again. With fresh eyes you start looking at existence. With love in the heart you approach life. With silence and innocence you penetrate your own innermost core. You are no longer just the head. Now you use the head, but it is your servant. First you become the heart, and then you transcend even the heart.

Going beyond thoughts and feelings and becoming a pure *isness* is maturity. Maturity is the ultimate flowering of meditation.

Jesus says, "Unless you are born again you will not enter into the kingdom of God." He is right, you have to be born again.

Once Jesus was standing in a marketplace and somebody asked, "Who is worthy of entering into your kingdom of God?" He looked around. There was a rabbi, and the rabbi must have moved forward a little, thinking that he would be chosen—but he was not chosen. There was the most virtuous man of the town—the moralist, the puritan. He moved forward a little, hoping that he would be chosen, but he was not chosen. Jesus looked around—he saw a small child, who was not expecting to be chosen, who had not moved, not even an inch. There was no idea, there was no question that he would be chosen. He was just enjoying the whole scene—the crowd and Jesus and people talking, and he was listening. Jesus called the child, he took the child up in his arms, and he said to the crowd, "Those who are like this small child, they are the only ones worthy of entering into the kingdom of God."

> Maturity means gaining your lost innocence again, reclaiming your paradise, becoming a child again. Of course it has a difference—the ordinary child is bound to be corrupted, but when you reclaim your childhood you become incorruptible.

But remember, he said, "Those who are *like* this small

child. . . ." He didn't say, "Those who are small children." There is a great difference between the two. He did not say, "This child will enter into the kingdom of God," because every child is bound to be corrupted, he has to go astray. Every Adam and every Eve is bound to be expelled from the garden of Eden, they have to go astray. That is the only way to regain real childhood: first you have to lose it. It is very strange, but that's how life is. It is very paradoxical, but life is a paradox. To know the real beauty of your childhood, first you have to lose it; otherwise you will never know it.

> ⤙
>
> Every Adam and every Eve is bound to be expelled from the garden of Eden, they have to go astray. That is the only way to regain real childhood: first you have to lose it.

The fish never knows where the ocean is—unless you pull the fish out of the ocean and throw it on the sand in the burning sun; then she knows where the ocean is. Now she longs for the ocean, she makes every effort to go back to the ocean, she jumps into the ocean. It is the same fish and yet not the same fish. It is the same ocean yet not the same ocean, because the fish has learned a new lesson. Now she is aware, now she knows, "This is the ocean and this is my life. Without it I am no more—I am part of it."

Every child has to lose his innocence and regain it. Losing is only half of the process—many have lost it, but very few have regained it. That is unfortunate, very unfortunate. Everybody loses it, but only once in a while does a Buddha, a Zarathustra, a Krishna, a Jesus regain it. Jesus is nobody else but Adam coming back home. Magdalene is nobody else but Eve coming back home. They have come out of the sea and they have seen the misery and they have seen the stupidity. They have seen that it is not blissful to be out of the ocean.

The moment you become aware that to be a part of any society, any religion, any culture is to remain miserable, is to remain a prisoner—that very day you start dropping your chains. Maturity is coming, you are gaining your innocence again.

MATURITY AND AGING

There is a great difference between maturity and aging, a vast difference, and people always remain confused about it. People think that to age is to become mature—but aging belongs to the body. Everybody is aging, everybody will become old, but not necessarily mature. Maturity is an inner growth.

Aging is nothing that you do, aging is something that happens physically. Every child born, when time passes, becomes old. Maturity is something that you bring to your life—it comes out of awareness. When a person ages with full awareness, he becomes mature. Aging plus awareness, experiencing plus awareness, is maturity.

You can experience a thing in two ways. You can simply experience it as if you are hypnotized, unaware, not attentive to what is happening; the thing happened but you were not there. It didn't happen in your presence, you were absent. You just passed by, it never struck any note in you. It never left any mark on you, you never learned anything from it. It may have become part of your memory, because in a way you were present, but it never became your wisdom. You never grew through it. Then you are aging.

But if you bring the quality of awareness to an experience the same experience becomes maturity.

> Aging is nothing that you do, aging is something that happens physically. Every child born, when time passes, becomes old. Maturity is something that you bring to your life—it comes out of awareness.

There are two ways to live: one, to live in a deep sleep—then you age, every moment you become old, every moment you go on dying, that's all. Your whole life consists of a long, slow death. But if you bring awareness to your experiences—whatsoever you do, whatsoever happens to you, you are alert, watchful, mindful, you are savoring the experience from all the corners, you are trying to understand the meaning of it, you are trying to penetrate the very depth of it, what has happened to you, you are trying to live it intensely and totally—then it is not just a surface phenomenon. Deep down within you something is changing with it. You are becoming more alert. If this is a mistake, this experience, you will never commit it again.

A mature person never commits the same mistake again. But a person who is just old goes on committing the same mistakes again and again. He lives in a circle; he never learns anything. You will be angry today, you were angry yesterday and the day before yesterday, and tomorrow you are going to be angry and the day after tomorrow also. Again and again you get angry, again and again you repent, again and again you make a deep decision that you are not going to do it again. But that decision makes no change—whenever you are disturbed the rage takes over, you are possessed; the same mistake is committed. You are aging.

If you live an experience of anger totally, never again will you be angry. One experience will be enough to teach that it is foolish, that it is absurd, that it is simply stupid—not that it is a sin, it is simply stupid. You are harming yourself and harming others, for nothing. The thing is not worth it. Then you are getting mature. Tomorrow the situation will be repeated but anger will not be repeated. And a man who is gaining in maturity has not *decided* that he will not be angry again, no—that is the sign of a man who is not getting mature. A man of maturity never decides for the future; the maturity itself takes care. You live today—that very living will decide how the tomorrow is going to be; it will come out of it.

> A mature person never commits the same mistake again. But a person who is just old goes on committing the same mistakes again and again. He lives in a circle, he never learns anything.

If the anger was painful, poisonous, you suffered hell through it, what is the point of deciding or taking a vow and going to the temple and declaring, "Now I take a vow that I will never be angry again"? All this is childish, there is no point! If you have known that anger is poisonous, it is finished! That way is closed, that door no longer exists for you. The situation will be repeated tomorrow but you will not be possessed by the situation. You have learned something—that understanding will be there. You may even laugh, you may even enjoy the whole thing of how people get so foolish. Your understanding is growing through every experience.

You can live life as if you are in hypnosis—that's how ninety-nine percent of people live—or you can live with intensity, awareness. If you live with awareness, you mature; otherwise you simply become old. And to become old is not to become wise. If you have been a fool when you were young and now you have become old, you will be just an old fool, that's all. Just becoming old, you cannot become wise. You may be even more foolish because you may have clung to mechanical habits, robotlike.

> A man of maturity never decides for the future, the maturity itself takes care. You live today—that very living will decide how the tomorrow is going to be, it will come out of it.

Life can be lived in two ways. If you live unconsciously you simply die; if you live consciously you attain more and more life. Death will come—but it never comes to a mature man, it comes only to a man who has been aging and getting old. A mature person never dies, because he will learn even through death. Even death is going to be an experience to be intensely lived, and watched, allowed.

A mature man never dies. In fact, on the rock of maturity death struggles and shatters itself, commits suicide. Death dies, but never a mature man. That is the message of all the awakened ones, that you are deathless. They have known it, they have lived their death. They have watched and they have found that it can surround you but you remain aloof, you remain far away. Death happens near you but it never happens to you.

Deathless is your being, blissful is your being, divine is your being, but those experiences you cannot cram into the mind and the memory. You have to pass through life and attain them. Much suffering is there, much pain is there. And because of pain and suffering people like to live stupidly—it has to be understood why so many people insist that they should live in hypnosis, why Buddhas and Christs go on telling people to be awake, and nobody listens. There must be some deep involvement in the hypnosis, there must be some deep investment. What is the investment?

> To become old is not to become wise. If you have been a fool when you were young and now you have become old, you will be just an old fool, that's all.

The mechanism has to be understood; otherwise you will listen to me and you will never become aware. You will listen and you will make it a part of your knowledge, that "Yes, this man says be aware and it is good to be aware, and those who attain to awareness become mature. . . ." But you yourself will not attain to it, it will remain just knowledge. You may communicate your knowledge to others, but nobody is helped that way.

Why? Have you ever asked this question? Why don't you attain to awareness? If it leads to the infinite bliss, to the attainment of *satchitananda,* to absolute truth—then why not be aware? Why do you insist on being sleepy? There is some investment, and this is the investment: if you become aware, there is suffering. If you become aware, you become aware of pain, and the pain is so much that you would like to take a tranquilizer and be asleep.

This sleepiness in life works as a protection against pain. But this is the trouble—if you are asleep against pain, you are asleep against pleasure also. Think of it as if there are two faucets: on one is written "pain" and on the other is written "pleasure." You would like to close the faucet on which pain is written, and you would like to open the faucet on which pleasure is written. But this is the game—if you close the pain faucet the pleasure faucet immediately closes, because behind both there is only one faucet, on which "awareness" is written. Either both remain open or both remain closed, because both are two faces of the same phenomenon, two aspects.

> A mature person never dies, because he will learn even through death. Even death is going to be an experience to be intensely lived, and watched, allowed.

And this is the whole contradiction of mind: mind wants to be more and more happy—happiness is possible if you are aware. And then mind wants to be less and less in pain—but less and less pain is possible only if you are *unaware.* Now you are in a dilemma. If you want no pain, immediately pleasure disappears from your life, happiness disappears. If you want happiness you open the faucet—immediately there is pain also flowing. If you are aware, you have to be aware of both. Life is pain and pleasure. Life is happiness and unhappiness. Life is day and night, life is life and death. You have to be aware of both.

So remember it. If you are afraid of pain you will remain in hypnosis; you will age, become old, and die. You missed an opportunity. If you want to be aware then you have to be aware of both pain and pleasure; they are not separate phenomena. And a man who becomes aware becomes very happy but also becomes capable of deep unhappiness, of which you are not capable.

It happened, a Zen Master died and his chief disciple—who was a famous man on his own, even more famous than the Master; in fact the Master had become famous because of the disciple—started crying; sitting on the steps of the temple he started crying with tears flowing down. Thousands of people had gathered; they could not believe it, because you never see any awakened man crying and weeping with tears rolling down his face. They said, "We cannot believe it—what is hap-

> Life is happiness and unhappiness. Life is day and night, life is life and death. You have to be aware of both.

pening? You are crying, and you yourself have been saying to us that the innermost being never dies, that death does not exist. We have heard you say millions of times that death does not exist—so why are you crying? Your Master is still alive in his being."

The disciple opened his eyes and he said, "Don't disturb me. Let me cry and weep. I'm not crying for the Master and his being, I am crying for his body. His body was also beautiful. Never again will that body exist."

And then somebody tried to persuade him that this would create a bad name for him: "So many people have gathered, and they will think that you are not enlightened."

The disciple said, "Let them think whatsoever they want to think. Since the day I became enlightened I have become infinitely blissful, but I have also become infinitely sensitive to pain and suffering."

This seems to be as it should be. If you hit Buddha, Buddha will suffer more than you will if somebody hits you—because he has become infinitely sensitive. His sensitivity is very delicate, he is just like a lotus petal. Your stone will hit him very deeply, it will give him deep suffering. Of course he will be aware of it, of course he will be aloof from it. Of course he will be transcendental to it, he will be knowing that it is happening and he will not be a part of it, he will be a cloudlike phenomenon surrounding it—but it is happening.

You cannot be so sensitive to pain, you are so fast asleep. You move like a drunkard—the drunkard falls on the street, hits his head in the gutter, nothing happens. If he were aware there would have been pain.

Buddha suffers infinitely and Buddha enjoys infinitely. Always remember, whenever you reach to a high peak, a deep valley is being created simultaneously. If you want to reach to the heavens, your roots will have to go to the very hell. Because you are afraid of pain you cannot become aware—and then you cannot learn anything.

It is just as if you are so afraid of enemies that you have closed the doors of your house. Now even the friend cannot enter, even the lover is left out. The lover goes on knocking on the door but you are afraid, maybe it is the enemy. So you are closed—that's how I see you all, closed, afraid of the enemy, and the friend cannot enter. You have turned the friend into an enemy—now nobody can enter, you are so afraid.

Open the door. When the fresh air enters the house there is every possibility of dangers also entering. When the friend comes, the enemy comes also because day and night enter together, pain and pleasure enter together, life and death enter together. Don't be afraid of pain, otherwise you will live in anesthesia. The surgeon gives an anesthetic before he operates on you because there is going to be much pain, you will not be able to tolerate it. Your consciousness has to be dimmed, darkened, then he can cut your whole body and you will not suffer.

Because of the fear of pain you have forced yourself to live in a dim consciousness, in a dimmed existence, almost not alive—this is the fear. You have to drop that fear, you have to face pain, you have to move through suffering—only then the possibility opens for the friend to enter.

And when you know both, you immediately become the third. When you know both—pain and pleasure, the duality, the day and night—suddenly you have become transcendental.

Maturity is awareness. Aging is just wasting yourself.

THE MOST FUNDAMENTAL THING TO BE REMEMBERED is that life is dialectical. It exists through duality, it is a rhythm between opposites. You cannot be happy forever, otherwise happiness will lose all meaning. You cannot be in harmony forever, otherwise you will become unaware of the harmony. Harmony has to be followed by discord again and again, and happiness has to be followed by unhappiness. Every pleasure has its own pain, and every pain has its own pleasure.

Unless one understands this duality of existence, one remains in unnecessary misery.

Accept the total, with all its agonies and all its ecstasies. Don't hanker for the impossible; don't desire that there should be only ecstasy and no agony. Ecstasy cannot exist alone, it needs a contrast. Agony becomes the blackboard, then ecstasy becomes very clear and loud, just as in the darkness of night the stars are so bright. The darker is the night the brighter are the stars. In the day they don't disappear, they simply become invisible; you cannot see them because there is no contrast.

> Accept the total, with all its agonies and all its ecstasies. Don't hanker for the impossible, don't desire that there should be only ecstasy and no agony.

Think of a life without death; it will be unendurable pain, an unendurable existence. It will be impossible to live without death—death defines life, gives it a kind of intensity. Because life is fleeting, each moment becomes precious. If life is eternal, then who cares? One can wait for tomorrow forever—then who will live now and here? Because tomorrow there is death, it forces you to live now and here. You have to plunge into the present moment, you have to go to its ultimate depth because who knows? The next moment may come, may not come.

Seeing this rhythm one is at ease, at ease with both. When

unhappiness comes one welcomes it, when happiness comes one welcomes it, knowing that they are partners in the same game. This is something that has to be continuously remembered. If it becomes a fundamental remembrance in you, your life will have a totally new flavor—the flavor of freedom, the flavor of unclingingness, the flavor of nonattachment. Whatsoever comes you remain still, silent, accepting.

And the person who is capable of being still, silent, accepting of pain, frustration, and misery, transforms the very quality of misery itself. To him, misery also becomes a treasure; to him, even pain gives a sharpness. To him, even darkness has its own beauty, depth, infinity. To him, even death is not the end but only a beginning of something unknown.

MATURITY OF SPIRIT

The qualities of a mature person are very strange. First, he is not a person. He is no longer a self—he has a presence, but he is not a person.

Second, he is more like a child, simple and innocent. That's why I said the qualities of a mature person are very strange, because maturity gives a sense as if he has experienced, as if he is aged, old—physically he may be old, but spiritually he is an innocent child. His maturity is not just experience gained through life—then he would not be like a child, then he would not be a presence—he would be an experienced person, knowledgeable but not mature.

Maturity has nothing to do with your life experiences. It has something to do with your inward journey, your experiences of the inner.

The more a man goes deeper into himself the more mature he is. When he has reached the very center of his being he is perfectly mature. But at that moment the person disappears, only presence remains. The self disappears, only silence remains. Knowledge disappears, only innocence remains.

> The person who is capable of being still, silent, accepting of pain, frustration, and misery, transforms the very quality of misery itself. To him, misery also becomes a treasure; to him, even pain gives a sharpness. To him, even darkness has its own beauty, depth, infinity.

To me, maturity is another name for realization: you have come to the fulfillment of your potential, it has become actual. The seed has come on a long journey and has blossomed.

Maturity has a fragrance. It gives a tremendous beauty to the individual. It gives intelligence, the sharpest possible intelligence. It makes him nothing but love. His action is love, his inaction is love; his life is love, his death is love. He is just a flower of love.

The West has definitions of maturity that are very childish. The West means by maturity that you are no longer innocent, that you have ripened through life experiences, that you cannot be cheated easily, that you cannot be exploited, that you have within you something like a solid rock, a protection, a security. This definition is very ordinary, very worldly. Yes, in the world you will find mature people of this type. But the way I see maturity is totally different, diametrically opposite to this definition. The maturity I am talking about will not make you a rock; it will make you so vulnerable, so soft, so simple.

I remember . . . A thief entered a mystic's hut. It was a full-moon night, and by mistake he had entered; otherwise, what can you find in a mystic's house? The thief was looking and was amazed that there was nothing—and then suddenly he saw a man who was coming with a candle in his hand. The man said, "What are you looking for in the dark? Why did you not wake me up? I was just sleeping near the front door, and I could have showed you the whole house." And he looked so simple and so innocent, as if he could not conceive that anybody could be a thief.

> Maturity has nothing to do with your life experiences. It has something to do with your inward journey, your experiences of the inner. The more a man goes deeper into himself the more mature he is.

In the face of such simplicity and innocence the thief said, "Perhaps you do not know that I am a thief."

The mystic said, "That doesn't matter, everybody has to be someone. The point is that I have been in the house for thirty years and I have not found anything, so let us search together! And if we can find something we can be partners. I have not found anything in this house—it is just empty." The thief was a little afraid—the man seems to be strange! Either he is mad or . . . who knows what kind of man he is? He wanted to escape, and besides he had brought things from two other houses that he had left outside the house.

The mystic had only one blanket—that was all that he had—and it was a cold night, so he told that thief, "Don't leave in this way, don't insult me this way; otherwise I will never be able to forgive myself, that a poor man came to my house in the middle of the night and had to go empty-handed. Just take this blanket. And it will be good—outside it is so cold. I am inside the house; it is warmer here."

He covered the thief with his blanket. The thief was just losing his mind! He said, "What are you doing? I am a thief!"

The mystic said, "That does not matter. In this world everybody has to be somebody, has to do something. You may be stealing, that doesn't matter—a profession is a profession. Just do it well, with all my blessings. Do it perfectly, don't be caught; otherwise you will be in trouble."

The thief said, "You are strange. You are naked, and you don't have anything. . . ."

The mystic said, "Don't be worried, because I am coming with you! Only the blanket was keeping me in this house; otherwise in this house there is nothing—and the blanket I have given to you. I am coming with you—we will live together! And you seem to have many things; it is a good partnership. I have given my all to you, you can give me a little bit—that will be right."

The thief could not believe it. He just wanted to escape from that place and from that man. He said, "No, I cannot take you with me. I have my wife, I have my children. And my neighbors, what will they say if I bring a naked man to my house . . . ?"

The mystic said, "That's right. I will not put you in any embarrassing situation. So you can go, I will remain in this house." And as the thief was going, the mystic shouted, "Hey! Come back!" The thief had never heard such a strong voice; it went just like a knife. He had to come back. The mystic said, "Learn some ways of courtesy. I have given you the blanket and you have not even thanked me. So first, thank me—it will help you a long way. Second, going out . . . you opened the door when you came in—close the door! Can't you see the night is so cold, and can't you see that I have given you the blanket and I am naked? Your being a thief is okay, but as far as manners are concerned, I am a difficult man. I cannot tolerate this kind of behavior. Say thank you!"

The thief had to say, "Thank you, sir," and he closed the door and escaped. He could not believe what had happened! He could not sleep the whole night. Again and again he remembered . . . he had never heard such a strong voice, such power. And the man had nothing!

He inquired the next day and he found out that this man was a great Master. He had not done well—it was absolutely ugly to go to that poor man, he had nothing. But he was a great Master.

The thief said, "That I can understand myself—he is a very strange kind of man. In my whole life I have been coming in contact with different kinds of people, from the poorest to the richest, but never . . . even remembering him, a shivering goes through my body. When he called me back I could not run away. I was absolutely free, I could have taken the things and run away but I could not. There was something in his voice that pulled me back."

After a few months the thief was caught, and in the court the magistrate asked him, "Can you name a person who knows you in this vicinity?"

He said, "Yes, one person knows me," and he named the Master.

The magistrate said, "That's enough—call the Master. His testimony is worth that of ten thousand people. What he says about you will be enough to give judgment."

The magistrate asked the Master, "Do you know this man?"

He said, "Know him? We are partners! He is my friend, he even visited me one night in the middle of the night. It was so cold that I gave him my blanket. He is using it, you can see. That blanket is famous all over the country; everybody knows it is mine."

The magistrate said, "He is your friend? And does he steal?"

The Master said, "Never! He can never steal. He is such a gentleman that when I gave him the blanket he said to me, 'Thank you, sir.' When he went out of the house, he silently closed the door. He is a very polite, nice fellow."

The magistrate said, "If you say so, then all the testimonies of the witnesses who have said that he is a thief are canceled. He is freed." The mystic went out and the thief followed him.

The mystic said, "What are you doing? Why are you coming with me?"

He said, "Now I can never leave you. You have called me your friend, you have called me your partner. Nobody has ever given me any respect. You are the first person who has said that

I am a gentleman, a nice person. I am going to sit at your feet and learn how to be like you. From where have you got this maturity, this power, this strength, this seeing of things in a totally different way?"

The mystic said, "Do you know that night how bad I felt? You had gone—it was so cold without a blanket that sleep was not possible. I was just sitting by the window watching the full moon, and I wrote a poem: 'If I were rich enough I would have given this perfect moon to that poor fellow, who had come in the dark to search for something in a poor man's house. I would have given the moon if I had been rich enough, but I am poor myself.' I will show you the poem, come with me.

"I wept that night, that thieves should learn a few things. At least they should inform a day or two ahead when they come to a man like me so we can arrange something, so they don't have to go empty-handed. And it is good that you remembered me in the court; otherwise those fellows are dangerous, they might have mistreated you. I offered that very night to come with you and be partners with you, but you refused. Now you want to come with me! There is no problem, you can come; whatever I have I will share with you. But it is not material, it is something invisible."

The thief said, "That I can feel—it is something invisible. But you have saved my life, and now my life is yours. Make whatever you want to make of it, I have been simply wasting it. Seeing you, looking in your eyes, one thing is certain—that you can transform me. I have fallen in love from that very night."

Maturity to me is a spiritual phenomenon.

MATURITY OF SPIRIT IS TOUCHING YOUR INNER SKY. Once you settle down in your inner sky, you have found a home, and a great maturity arises in your actions, in your behavior. Then whatever you do has grace in it. Then whatever you do is a poem in itself. You live poetry, your walking becomes dancing, your silence becomes music.

By maturity is meant that you have come home. You are no longer a child who has to grow—you have grown up. You have touched the height of your potential. For the first time in a strange sense you are not—and you *are*. You are not in your old ideas, imaginations, in your old comprehension of yourself; all that has gone down the drain. Now something new arises in you, absolutely new and virgin, which transforms your whole life into joy. You have become a stranger to the miserable world, you don't create misery for yourself or for anybody else. You live your life in total freedom, without any consideration for what others will say.

The people who are always considering others and their opinions are immature. They are dependent on the opinions of others. They can't do anything authentically, honestly they can't say what

> By maturity is meant that you have come home. You are no longer a child who has to grow—you have grown up. You have touched the height of your potential.

they want to say—they say what others want to hear. Your politicians say the things you want to hear. They give you the promises you want. They know perfectly well that they cannot fulfill these promises; neither is there any intent to fulfill them. But if they say exactly, truthfully, what the situation is, and make it clear to you that many of the things you are asking for are impossible, that they cannot be done, they will be thrown out of power. You will not choose a politician who is honest.

It is a very strange world. It is almost an insane asylum. <u>If, in this insane asylum, you become alert and aware of your inner being, you are blessed.</u>

> The people who are always considering others and their opinions are immature. They can't do anything authentically, honestly; they can't say what they want to say—they say what others want to hear.

THE SEVEN-YEAR CYCLES
OF LIFE

꙳

L ife has an inner pattern, it is good to understand it. Every seven years, physiologists say, the body and mind go through a crisis and a change. Every seven years all the cells of the body change, are completely renewed. In fact if you live seventy years, the average limit, your body dies ten times. Each seventh year everything changes—it is just like changing seasons. In seventy years the circle is complete. The line that moves from birth comes to death, the circle is complete in seventy years. It has ten divisions.

In fact man's life should not be divided into childhood, youth, old age. That is not very scientific, because every seven years a new age begins, a new step is taken.

For the first seven years a child is self-centered, as if he is the center of the whole world. The whole family moves around him. Whatsoever are his needs, they are to be fulfilled immediately; otherwise he will go into a tantrum, anger, rage. He lives like an emperor, a real emperor—the mother, the father, all are servants, and the whole family just exists for him. And of course he thinks the same is true for the wider world. The moon rises for him, the sun rises for him, the seasons change for him. A child for seven years remains absolutely egoistic, self-centered. If you ask psychologists they will say a child for seven years remains masturbatory, satisfied with himself. He does not need anything, anybody. He feels complete.

After seven years, a breakthrough. The child is no longer self-centered; he becomes eccentric, literally. *Eccentric*—the word means "going out of the center." He moves toward others. The other becomes the important phenomenon—friends, gangs . . . Now he is not so much interested in himself; he is interested in the other, the bigger world. He enters into an adventure to know who is this "other." Inquiry starts.

After the seventh year the child becomes a great questioner. He questions everything. He becomes a great skeptic because his inquiry is there. He asks millions of questions. He bores the parents to death, he becomes a nuisance. He is interested in the other, and everything of the world is his interest. Why are the trees green? Why did God create the world? Why is this so? He starts becoming more and more philosophic—inquiry, skepticism, he insists on going into things.

> For the first seven years a child is self-centered. Whatsoever are his needs, they are to be fulfilled immediately, otherwise he will go into a tantrum, anger, rage.

He kills a butterfly to see what is inside, destroys a toy just to see how it works, throws a clock just to look into it, how it goes on ticking and chiming—what is going on inside? He becomes interested in the other—but the other remains of the same sex. He is not interested in girls. If other boys are interested in girls he will think they are sissies. Girls are not interested in boys. If some girl is interested in boys and plays with them she is a tomboy, not normal, not average; something is wrong. This second stage psychoanalysts and psychologists will say is homosexual.

After the fourteenth year a third door opens. He is no longer interested in boys, girls are no longer interested in girls. They are polite, but not interested. That's why any friendship that happens between the seventh year and the fourteenth is the deepest, because the mind is homosexual, and never again in life will such friendship happen. Those friends remain friends forever, it was such a deep tie. You will become friendly with people but that will remain acquaintance, not that deep phenomenon that happened between the seventh and the fourteenth year.

But after the fourteenth year a boy is not interested in boys. If everything goes normally, if he is not stuck somewhere, he will be interested in girls. Now he is becoming heterosexual—not only interested in the others, but really *the other*—because when a boy is interested in boys, the boy may be "other" but he is still a boy just like himself, not exactly the other. When a boy becomes interested in girls, now he is really interested in the opposite, the real other. When a girl becomes interested in a boy, now the world enters.

The fourteenth year is a great revolutionary year. Sex becomes mature, one starts thinking in terms of sex; sexual fantasies become prominent in the dreams. The boy becomes a great Don Juan, starts courting. Poetry arises, romance. He is entering into the world.

By the twenty-first year—if everything goes normally, and a child is not forced by the society to do something which is not natural—by the twenty-first year a child becomes interested more in ambition than in love. He wants a Rolls-Royce, a great palace. He wants to be a success, a Rockefeller, a prime minister. Ambitions become prominent; desiring for the future, being a success, how to succeed, how to compete, how to move in the struggle is his whole concern.

Now he is not entering only the world of nature, he is entering the world of humanity, the marketplace. Now he is entering the world of madness. Now the market becomes the most prominent thing. His whole being goes toward the market—money, power, prestige.

If everything goes right—as it never goes, I am talking of the absolutely natural phenomenon—by the twenty-eighth year a man is not in any way trying to enter into an adventurous life. From twenty-one to twenty-eight one lives in adventure; by the twenty-eighth year one becomes more alert that all desires cannot be fulfilled. There is more understanding that many desires are impossible. If you are a fool you can go after them, but people who are intelligent enter another door by the twenty-eighth year. They become more interested in security and comfort, less in adventure and ambition. They start settling. The twenty-eighth year is the end of hippiedom.

At twenty-eight hippies become squares, revolutionaries are no longer revolutionaries; they start settling, they seek a comfortable life, a little bank balance. They don't want to be Rockefellers—that urge is no more. They want a small

> The fourteenth year is a revolutionary year. One starts thinking in terms of sex; sexual fantasies become prominent in the dreams. The boy becomes a great Don Juan, starts courting. Poetry arises, romance. He is entering into the world.

house, but established, a cozy place to live in, security, so at least this much they can always have, a little bank balance. They go to the insurance company nearabout the age of twenty-eight. They start settling. Now the vagabond is no more the vagabond. He purchases a house, starts living in it; he becomes civilized. The word *civilization* comes from the word *civis*, "citizen." Now he becomes part of a town, a city, an establishment. He is no more a vagabond, not a wanderer. Now he is not going to Kathmandu and Goa. He is not going anywhere—finished, traveled enough, known enough; now he wants to settle and rest a little.

> People go to the insurance company nearabout the age of twenty-eight. They start settling. Now the vagabond is no longer a vagabond.

By the thirty-fifth year life energy reaches its omega point. The circle is half complete and energies start declining. Now the man is not interested only in security and comfort, he becomes a Tory, orthodox. He becomes not only not interested in revolution, he becomes an anti-revolutionary. Now he is against all change, he is a conformist. He is against all revolutions; he wants the status quo because now he has settled and if anything changes the whole thing will unsettle. Now he is talking against hippies, against rebels; now he has become really a part of the establishment.

And this is natural—unless something goes wrong a man is not going to remain a hippie forever. That was a phase, good to pass through but bad to be stuck in. That means you remain stuck at a certain stage. It was good to be homosexual between seven and fourteen, but if one remains homosexual for his whole life that means he has not grown up, he is not adult. A woman has to be contacted, that is part of life. The other sex has to become important because only then will you be able to know the harmony of the opposites, the conflict, the misery, and the ecstasy—agony and ecstasy both. It is a training, a necessary training.

By the thirty-fifth year one has to become part of the conventional world. One starts believing in tradition, in the past, in the Vedas, the Koran, the Bible. One is absolutely against change because every change means your own life will be disturbed; now you have much to lose. You cannot be for revolution; you want to protect. One is in favor of the law and the courts and the government. One is no longer an anarchist; one is all for the government, rules, regulations, discipline.

By the forty-second year all sorts of physical and mental illnesses erupt, because now life is declining. Energy is moving toward death. As in the beginning—your energies were coming up and you were becoming more and more vital, energetic, you were becoming more and more strong—now just the opposite happens, you become weaker every day. But your habits persist. You have been eating enough up to the age of thirty-five; now if you continue your habit you will start gathering fat. Now, that much food is not needed. It was needed, but now it is not needed

> By the thirty-fifth year one is absolutely against change, because every change means your own life will be disturbed; now you have much to lose.

because life is moving toward death, it does not need that much food. If you go on filling your belly as you were doing before, then all sorts of illnesses will happen: high blood pressure, heart attack, insomnia, ulcers—they all happen nearabout forty-two; forty-two is one of the most dangerous points. Hair starts falling out, becoming gray. Life is turning into death.

And near the age of forty-two religion starts becoming important for the first time. You may have dabbled a little here and there in religion before, but now religion starts becoming for the first time important—because religion is deeply concerned with death. Now death is approaching and the first desire for religion arises.

Carl Gustav Jung has written that in his whole life he has been observing that people who come to him around the age of forty are always in need of religion. If they go mad, neurotic, psychotic, they cannot be helped unless they become deeply rooted in religion. They need religion; their basic need is religion. And if the society is secular and you have never been taught religion, the greatest difficulty comes nearabout the age of forty-two—because the society does not give you any avenue, any door, any dimension.

The society was good when you were fourteen, because the society gives enough of sex—the whole society is sexual; sex seems to be the only commodity hidden in every commodity. If you want to sell a ten-ton truck then too you have to use a naked woman. Or toothpaste—then too. Truck or toothpaste, it makes no difference: a naked woman is always smiling there behind. Really the *woman* is sold. The truck is not sold, the toothpaste is not sold—the woman is sold. And because the smile of the woman comes with the toothpaste, you have to purchase the toothpaste also. Everywhere sex is sold.

So this society, a secular society, is good for young people. But they are not going to remain young forever. When they become forty-two suddenly the society leaves them in limbo. They don't know what to do now. They go neurotic because they don't know, they have never been trained, no discipline has been given them to face death. The society has made them ready for life, but nobody has taught them to become ready for death. They need as much education for death as they need education for life.

If I were allowed my way then I would divide universities into two parts: one part for young people, another part for old people. Young people would come to learn the art of life—sex, ambition, struggle. Then when they became older and they reached the forty-two mark, they would again come back to the university to learn about death, God, meditation—because now the old universities won't be of any help to them. They need a new training, a new discipline, so that they can become anchored with the new phase that is happening to them.

> If the society is secular and you have never been taught religion, the greatest difficulty comes near the age of forty-two— because the society does not give you any avenue, any door, any dimension.

This society leaves them in limbo; that's why in the West there is so much mental illness. It is not so much in the East. Why? Because the East still gives a little training in religion. It has not disappeared completely; howsoever false, pseudo, it is still there, it exists just by the corner. No longer in the marketplace, no longer in the thick of life, just by the side—but there is a temple. Out of the way of life, but still it is there. You have to walk a few steps and you can go there, it still exists.

In the West religion is no longer part of life. Nearabout the age of forty-two every Westerner is going through psychological problems. Thousands of types of neuroses happen—and ulcers. Ulcers are the footprints of ambition. An ambitious man is bound to have ulcers in the stomach: ambition bites, it eats on you. An ulcer is nothing but eating yourself. You are so tense that you have started eating your own stomach lining. You are so tense, your stomach is so tense it never relaxes. Whenever the mind is tense the stomach is tense.

Ulcers are the footprints of ambition. If you have ulcers that shows you are a very successful man. If you have no ulcers you are a poor man; your life has been a failure, you failed utterly. If you have your first heart attack nearabout forty-two you are a great success. You must be at least a cabinet minister or a rich industrialist or a famous actor; otherwise, how will you explain the heart attack? A heart attack is the definition of success.

All successful people will have heart attacks, they have to. Their whole system is burdened with toxic elements: ambition, desire, future, tomorrow, which is never there. You lived in dreams, now your system cannot tolerate it anymore. And you remain so tense for the future that tension has become your very style of life. Now it is a deep-rooted habit.

At forty-two, again a breakthrough comes. One starts thinking about religion, the other world. Life seems to be too much, and so little time is left—how can you achieve God, nirvana, enlightenment? Hence the theory of reincarnation: "Don't be afraid. Again you will be born, again and again, and the wheel of life will go on moving and moving. Don't be afraid: there is enough time, there is enough eternity left—you can attain."

That's why in India three religions were born—Jainism, Buddhism, and Hinduism—and they don't agree on any other point except reincarnation. Such divergent theories, not even agreeing on the basic foundations of God, the nature of self . . . but they all three agree on the theory of reincarnation—there must be something to it. They all need time, because to attain Brahman—Hindus call it Brahman—much time is needed. It is such a great ambition, and only at the age of forty-two you become interested. Only twenty-eight years are left.

> An ambitious man is bound to have ulcers in the stomach: ambition bites, it eats on you. An ulcer is nothing but eating yourself. Ulcers are the footprints of ambition.

And this is just the beginning of the interest. In fact at the age of forty-two you become again a child in the world of religion and only twenty-eight years are left. Time seems too short, not enough at all to attain such great heights—Brahman, Hindus call it, Jainas call it moksha, absolute freedom from all past karmas. But thousands and millions of lives have been there in the past; within twenty-eight years how are you going to cope? How will you undo the whole past? Such a vast past is there, bad and good karmas—how are you going to clean your sins completely within twenty-eight years? It seems unjust! God is demanding too much, it is not possible. You will feel frustrated if only twenty-eight years are given to you. And Buddhists, who don't believe in God, don't believe in the soul—they also believe in re-incarnation. Nirvana, the final emptiness, the total emptiness . . . when you have remained filled with so much rubbish for so many lives, how are you going to unburden yourself within twenty-eight years? It is too much, seems an impossible task. So they all agree on one thing, that more future is needed, more time is needed.

Whenever you have ambition, time is needed. And to me a religious person is one who does not need time. He is liberated here and now, he achieves to the Brahman here and now, he is liberated, enlightened, here and now. A religious man does not need time at all because religion happens in a timeless moment. It happens now, it always happens now; it has never happened otherwise. In no other way has it ever happened.

At the age of forty-two the first urge arises, vague, not clear, confused. You are not even aware of what is happening, but you start looking at the temple with keen interest. Sometimes by the way, as a casual visitor, you come to the church also. Sometimes—having time, not doing anything—you start looking in the Bible, which has always been gathering dust on the table. Vague, not exactly clear, just like the small child who is vague about sex starts playing with his own sex organ, not knowing what he is doing. A vague urge . . . Sometimes one sits alone silently, suddenly feels peaceful, not knowing what he is doing. Sometimes one starts re-peating a mantra heard in childhood. The old grandmother used to do it; feeling tense, one starts repeating it. One starts seeking, searching for a guru, somebody to guide you. One takes initiation, starts learning a mantra, repeats it sometimes, then again forgets for a few days, again repeats . . . a vague search, groping.

By the forty-ninth year the search becomes clear; seven years it takes for the search to become clear. Now a determination arises. You are no longer interested in the others, particularly if everything has gone right—and I have to repeat this again and again because it never goes right—at the age of forty-nine one becomes uninterested in women. A woman becomes uninterested in men—the menopause, the forty-ninth year. The man doesn't feel like being sexual. The whole thing looks a little juvenile, the whole thing looks a little immature.

But the society can force things . . . In the East they have been against sex and they have suppressed sex. When the boy is fourteen they are suppressing sex and they want to believe that the boy is still a child, he doesn't think about girls. Other boys maybe—these boys can always be found in the neighborhood—but never your boy; he is innocent like a child, like an angel. And he *looks* very innocent, but it's not true—he fantasizes. The girl has entered his consciousness, has to enter, it is natural—and he has to hide it. He starts masturbating and he has to hide it. He has wet dreams and he has to hide it.

In the East a boy of fourteen becomes guilty. Something wrong is happening—only to him, because he cannot know that everybody everywhere is doing the same. And much is expected of him—that he should remain an angel, a virgin, not thinking about girls, not even dreaming about girls. But he has become interested—the society is suppressing him.

In the West this suppression has disappeared but another suppression has come—and this has to be understood because this is my feeling, that the society can never be nonsuppressive. If it drops one suppression, immediately it starts another. Now the suppression is near the age of forty-nine in the West: people are forced to remain in sex because the whole teaching says, "What are you doing? A man can be sexually potent up to the age of ninety!" Great authorities are saying it. And if you are not potent and you are not interested, you start feeling guilty. At the age of forty-nine a man starts feeling guilty that he is not making love as much as he should.

And there are teachers who go on teaching, "This is nonsense. You can make love, you can make love up to the age of ninety. Go on making love." And they say if you don't make love you will lose potency; if you continue then your organs continue functioning. If you stop then they will stop, and once you stop sex your life energy will drop, you will die soon. If the husband stops, the wife is after him: "What are you doing?" If the wife stops, the husband is after her: "This is against the psychologists and this may create some perversion."

> The society can never be nonsuppressive. If it drops one suppression, immediately it starts another. Now the suppression is near the age of forty-nine in the West: people are forced to remain in sex. A man starts feeling guilty that he is not making love as much as he should.

In the East we did one stupidity and in the West also, in the ancient days, they did the same stupidity. It was against religion for a child of fourteen to become sexually potent—and he becomes so naturally. The child cannot do anything, it is beyond his control. What can he do? How can he do it? All teaching about celibacy at the age of fourteen is stupid, you are suppressing the person. But the old authorities, traditions, gurus, old psychologists and religious people—they were all against sex, the whole authority was against sex. A child was suppressed, guilt was created. Nature was not allowed.

Now just the opposite is happening at the other end. At the age of forty-nine psychologists are forcing people to continue to make love; otherwise you will lose life. As at the age of fourteen sex naturally arises, so at the age of forty-nine it naturally subsides. It has to, because every circle has to be complete.

That's why in India we had decided that at the age of fifty man should start becoming a *vanprasth*, his eyes should move toward the forest, his back toward the marketplace. *Vanprasth* is a beautiful word; it means one who starts looking toward the Himalayas, toward the forest. Now his back is toward life and ambitions and desires and all that—finished. He starts moving toward aloneness, toward being himself.

> As at the age of fourteen sex naturally arises, so at the age of forty-nine it naturally subsides. It has to, because every circle has to be complete.

Before this, life was too much and he could not be alone; there were responsibilities to be fulfilled, children to be raised. Now they have become grown up. They are married—by the time you are forty-nine your children are getting married, settling. They are no longer hippies, they must be reaching the age of twenty-eight. They will settle—now you can unsettle. Now you can move beyond the home, you can become homeless. At the age of forty-nine one should start looking toward the forest, moving inward, becoming introverted, becoming more and more meditative and prayerful.

At the age of fifty-six again a change comes, a revolution. Now it is not enough to look toward the Himalayas; one has to really travel, one has to go. Life is ending, death is coming nearer. At the age of forty-nine one becomes uninterested in the other sex. At the age of fifty-six one should become uninterested in others, the society, the social formalities, the club. At the age of fifty-six one should resign from all Rotaries, all Lions; it looks foolish now, childish. Go to some Rotary Club or Lions Club and see people, dressed up with their ties and everything—it looks juvenile, childish. What are they doing? Lions—the very name looks foolish. For a small child, good—now they have for small children "Cub" clubs, and for women "Lioness" clubs. For cubs it is perfectly right, but for lions and lionesses . . . ? It shows that the minds are mediocre.

At the age of fifty-six one should be so mature as to come out of all social entanglements. Finished! One has lived enough, learned enough; now one gives thanks to everybody and comes out of it. Fifty-six is the time one should naturally become a sannyasin. One should take sannyas, one should renounce, it is natural—as you enter, so you should renounce. Life should have an entrance and it should also have an exit; otherwise it will be suffocating. You enter and you never come out and then you say you are suffocated, in agony. There is an exit, and that is sannyas—you come out of the society. You are not even interested in others by the age of fifty-six.

By the age of sixty-three you again become like a child, interested only in yourself. That is what meditation is—to be moving inward, as if everything else has fallen away and only you exist. Again you have become a child—of course very much enriched by life, very mature, understanding, with great intelligence. Now you again become innocent. You start moving inward. Only seven years are left, and you have to prepare for death. You have to be ready to die.

And what is the readiness to die? To die celebrating is the readiness to die. To die happy, joyfully, willingly, welcomingly, is to be ready. God gave you an opportunity to learn, and be, and you learned. Now you would like to rest. Now you would like to go to the ultimate home. It was a sojourn. You wandered in a strange land, you lived with strange people, you loved strangers and you learned much. Now the time has come: the prince must return to his own kingdom.

Sixty-three is the time when one becomes completely enclosed in oneself. The whole energy moves in and in and in, turning in. You become a circle of energy, not moving anywhere. No reading, not much talking. More and more silent, more and more with oneself, remaining totally independent of all that is around you. The energy by and by subsides.

By the age of seventy you are ready. And if you have followed this natural pattern, just before your death—nine months before your death—you will become aware that death is coming. As a child has to pass nine months in the mother's womb, the same circle is totally repeated, completely repeated, utterly repeated. By the time death comes, nine months before, you will become aware. Now you are entering the womb again. This womb is no longer in the mother, this womb is inside you.

Indians call the innermost shrine of a temple the *garbha*, the womb. When you go to a temple the innermost part of the temple is called the womb. It is very symbolically called so, very deliberately;

that is the womb one has to enter. In the last phase—nine months—one enters into oneself, one's own body becomes the womb. One moves to the innermost shrine where the flame has always been burning, where the light has always been, where the temple is, where the god has always been living. This is the natural process.

For this natural process, no future is needed. You have to be living naturally *this* moment. The next moment will come out of it on its own. Just as a child grows and becomes a youth—there is no need to plan for it, one simply becomes; it is natural, it happens. As a river flows and comes to the ocean—the same way—you flow and you come to the end, to the ocean. But one should remain natural, floating and in the moment. Once you start thinking about the future and ambition and desire, you are missing this moment. And this moment missed will create perversion because you will always lack something; a gap will be there.

If a child has not lived his childhood well, then that unlived childhood will enter into his youth—because where will it go? It has to be lived. When a child is at the age of four and dances and jumps and runs around, butterfly catching, it is beautiful. But when a young man of twenty runs after butterflies, he is crazy—then you have to admit him to the hospital, he is a mental case. Nothing was wrong with it at the age of four; it was just natural, it was the thing to do. It was the *right* thing to do—if a child is not running after butterflies something is wrong, he has to be taken to the psychoanalyst. Then it was okay. But when he is twenty and running after butterflies then you should suspect something has gone wrong, he has not grown up. The body has grown, the mind is lagging behind. It must be somewhere in his childhood—he was not allowed to live it completely. If he lives the childhood completely he will become a young man, beautiful, fresh, uncontaminated by the child-hood. He will shed the childhood as a snake sheds its old skin. He will come out of it fresh. He will have the intelligence of a young man and he won't look retarded.

Live youth completely. Don't listen to the ancient authorities, just drop them out of the way. Don't listen to them—because they have killed youth, they are suppressive of youth. They are against sex and if some society is against sex then sex will spread all over your life, it will become poison. Live it! Enjoy it!

Between the fourteenth and twenty-first year a boy is at his high-est peak of sexuality. In fact, near the age of seventeen or eighteen he reaches the peak of sexuality. Never again will he be so potent, and if those moments are missed he will never achieve the beautiful orgasm that could have been achieved near the age of seventeen or eighteen.

> You have to be living naturally *this* moment. The next moment will come out of it on its own. Just as a child grows and becomes a youth—there is no need to plan for it, one simply becomes, it is natural, it happens.

I am in a difficulty continuously, because the society forces you to remain celibate at least up to the twenty-first year—that means the greatest possibility of achieving sex, learning sex, entering sex will be missed. By the time you reach twenty-one, twenty-two, you are already old as far as sex is con-cerned. Near the age of seventeen you were at the peak—so potent, so powerful, that the orgasm, the sexual orgasm, would have spread to your very cells. Your whole body would have taken a bath of eternal bliss. And when I say sex can become samadhi, superconsciousness, I don't say it for people who are seventy, remember! I am saying it for people who are seventeen. About my book *From Sex to Superconsciousness* . . . old men come to me and they say, "We have read your book but we never achieve anything like this." How can you? You have missed the time, and it cannot be replaced. And I am not responsible; your society is responsible and you listened to it.

> When I say sex can become samadhi, superconsciousness, I don't say it for people who are seventy, remember! I am saying it for people who are seventeen.

If between the ages of fourteen and twenty-one a child is allowed to have free sex, absolutely free sex, he will never bother about sex. He will be completely free. He will not look at *Playboy* and *Playgirl* magazines. He will not hide ugly, obscene pictures in the cupboard or in the Bible. He will not go out of his way to throw things at women, he will not become a bottom pincher. These things are ugly, simply ugly—but you go on tolerating them and not feeling what is happening, why everybody is neurotic.

Once you find a chance to rub against a woman's body you never miss it—what ugliness! Rubbing against a body?—something has remained unfulfilled in you. And when an old man looks with lustful eyes, there is nothing compared to that; it is the most ugly thing in the world when an old man looks with lust in his eyes. His eyes should be innocent now, he must be finished by now. Not that sex is something ugly, remember—I am not saying sex is ugly. Sex is beautiful at its own time and season, and sex is ugly out of season, out of time. Sex is a disease when it is in a ninety-year-old man. That's why people say "dirty old man." It *is* dirty.

A young man is beautiful, sexual. He shows vitality, life. An old man, sexual, shows unlived life, an empty life, immature. He missed the opportunity and now he cannot do anything, but he goes on thinking, rambling in the mind about sex, fantasizing.

Remember, between the fourteenth and the twenty-first year a right society will allow absolute freedom for sex. And then society will become less sexual automatically; beyond a certain time there will be no sex. The disease will not be there—live sex when the moment is ripe and forget it when the moment has gone. But that you can do only if you have lived; otherwise you cannot forget and you cannot forgive. You will cling, it will become a wound inside.

> If between the ages of fourteen and twenty-one a child is allowed to have free sex, absolutely free sex, he will never bother about sex. He will be completely free. He will not look at *Playboy* and *Playgirl* magazines. He will not hide ugly, obscene pictures in the cupboard or in the Bible.

In the East don't listen to the authorities, whatsoever they say. Listen to nature—when nature says it is time to love, love. When nature says it is time to renounce, renounce. And don't listen to the foolish psychoanalysts and psychologists in the West. Howsoever refined instruments they have—Masters and Johnson and others—and however many vaginas they have been testing and examining, they don't know life.

> A young man is beautiful, sexual. He shows vitality, life. An old man, sexual, shows unlived life, an empty life, immature. He missed the opportunity and now he cannot do anything but he goes on thinking, rambling in the mind about sex.

In fact I suspect that these Masterses and Johnsons and Kinseys are voyeurs. They themselves are ill about sex; otherwise who bothers to watch one thousand vaginas with instruments—watching what is happening inside when a woman makes love? Who bothers? What nonsense! But when things go perverted then these types of things happen. Now the Masterses and Johnsons have become the experts, the final authorities. If you are having any sexual problem, then they are the final authority to go to. And I suspect they have missed their youth, they have not lived their sex life rightly. Somewhere something is lacking and they are fulfilling it through such tricks.

And when a thing is in the garb of science, you can do anything. Now they have made false, electric penises, and those electric penises go on throbbing in the real vaginas, and they go on trying to find what is happening inside, whether orgasm is clitoral or vag-

inal, or what hormones are flowing, what hormones are not flowing, and how long a woman can make love. They say to the very
end—on her deathbed a woman can make love.

In fact their suggestion is that after the menopause a woman can
make better love than ever—that
means after the forty-ninth year.
Why do they say that? Because, they
say, before the forty-ninth year a
woman is always afraid of getting
pregnant. Even if she is on the pill, no
pill is a hundred percent proof; there
is a fear. By the forty-ninth year,
when the menopause comes and the
period stops, then there is no fear; a
woman is completely free. If their
teaching spreads women are going to
become vampires, and old women
will chase men because they are unafraid now and the authority sanc-
tions it. In fact they say that then it is
the right time to enjoy—without any
responsibility.

> I suspect that these
> Masterses and
> Johnsons and Kinseys
> are voyeurs. They
> themselves are ill
> about sex, otherwise
> who bothers to watch
> one thousand vaginas
> with instruments—
> watching what is
> happening inside when
> a woman makes love?
> Who bothers?

And for men also, they go on
saying the same thing. They have
come across a man who in his sixtieth
year can make love five times a day. This man seems to be a freak.
Something is wrong with his hormones and his body. At the age
of sixty! He is not natural, because as I see it—and this I am saying
out of my own experience in many lives, I can remember them—by

the forty-ninth year a natural man is not interested in women; the interest goes. As it comes, it goes.

Everything that comes has to go. Everything that arises has to fall. Every wave that arises has to disappear, there must be a time when it goes. At fourteen it comes; at forty-nine or thereabouts it goes. But a man making love five times a day at the age of sixty—something is wrong. Something is very, very wrong; his body is not functioning rightly. It is the other end of impotence, the other extreme. When a boy of fourteen does not feel any sex, or a young man of eighteen has no desire, something is wrong—he has to be treated. When a man of sixty needs to make love five times a day, something is wrong. His body has gone berserk; it is not functioning rightly, naturally.

If you live in the moment totally then there is no need to worry for the future. A rightly lived childhood brings you to a right, ripe youth—flowing, vital, alive, a wild ocean of energy. A rightly lived youth brings you to the very settled, calm, and quiet life. A calm and quiet life brings you to a religious inquiry: What is life? Living is not enough, one has to penetrate the mystery. A calm and quiet life brings you to meditative moments. Meditation brings you to renounce all that is useless now, just junk, garbage. The whole life becomes garbage; only one thing remains always, eternally valuable, and that is your awareness.

By the time of the seventieth year, when you are ready to die—if you lived everything rightly, in the moment, never postponing for the future, never dreaming for the future, you lived it totally in the moment whatsoever it was—nine months before your death you will become aware. You have attained so much awareness, you can see that now death is coming.

Many saints have declared their deaths ahead of time, but I have not come across a single instance when the death was declared before nine months. Exactly nine months before, a man of awareness, uncluttered with the past . . . because one who never thinks of the future will never think of the past. They are together; the past and future are together, joined together. When you think of the future it is nothing but the projection of the past; when you think of the past it is nothing but trying to plan for the future—they are together. The present is outside of both—a man who lives in this moment now and here is not cluttered with the past and not cluttered with the future, he remains unburdened. He has no burden to carry, he moves without weight. The gravitation doesn't affect him. In fact, he doesn't walk, he flies. He has wings. Before he dies, exactly nine months before, he will become aware that death is coming.

> A man who lives in this moment, now and here, is not cluttered with the past and not cluttered with the future, remains unburdened. He has no burden to carry, he moves without weight. Gravity doesn't affect him. In fact, he doesn't walk, he flies. He has wings.

And he will enjoy and he will celebrate and he will say to people, "My ship is coming, and I am only for a little while longer on this bank. Soon I will be going to my home. This life has been beautiful, a strange experience. I loved, learned, lived much, I am enriched. I had come here with nothing and I am going with much experience, much maturity." He will be thankful to all that has happened—good and bad both, right and wrong both, because from *every*thing he learned. Not only from right, from wrong also—sages that he came across, he learned from them, and sinners, yes, from them also. They all helped. People who robbed him helped, people who helped him helped. People who were friends helped, people who were enemies helped—everyone helped. Summer and winter, satiety and hunger, everything helped. One can be thankful to all.

When one is thankful to all and ready to die, celebrating for this opportunity that one was given, death becomes beautiful. Then death is not the enemy, it is the greatest friend because it is the crescendo of life. It is the highest peak that life achieves. It is not the end of life, it is the climax. It looks like the end because you have never known life—to one who has known life it appears as the very crescendo, the very peak, the highest peak.

> When one is thankful to all and ready to die, celebrating for this opportunity that one was given, death becomes beautiful. Then death is not the enemy, it is the greatest friend because it is the crescendo of life. It is the highest peak that life achieves.

Death is the culmination, the fulfillment. Life does not end in it; in fact life flowers in it—it is the flower. But to know the beauty of death one has to be ready for it, one has to learn the art.

THE MATURE
RELATIONSHIP

～

DEPENDENCE, INDEPENDENCE, INTERDEPENDENCE

L ove can have three dimensions. One is that of dependence; that's what happens to the majority of people. The husband is dependent on the wife, the wife is dependent on the husband; they exploit each other, they dominate each other, they possess each other, they reduce each other to a commodity. In ninety-nine percent of cases, that's what is happening in the world. That's why love, which can open the gates of paradise, opens only the gates of hell.

The second possibility is love between two independent persons. That too happens once in a while. But that too brings misery, because there is constant conflict. No adjustment is possible; both are so independent and nobody is ready to compromise, to adjust with the other.

Poets, artists, thinkers, scientists, those who live in a kind of independence, at least in their minds, are impossible people to live with; they are eccentric people to live with. They give freedom to the other, but their freedom looks more like indifference than like freedom, looks more as if they don't care, as if it doesn't matter to them. They leave each other to their own spaces. Relationship seems to be only superficial; they are afraid to go deeper into each other because they are more attached to their freedom than to love, and they don't want to compromise.

And the third possibility is of interdependence. That happens very rarely, but whenever it happens a part of paradise falls on the earth. Two persons, neither independent nor dependent but in a tremendous synchronicity, as if breathing for each other, one soul in two bodies—whenever that happens, love has happened. Call only this love. The other two are not really love, they are just arrangements—social, psychological, biological, but arrangements. The third is something spiritual.

> Poets, artists, thinkers, scientists, those who live in a kind of independence, at least in their minds, are impossible people to live with; they are eccentric people to live with. They give freedom to the other, but their freedom looks more like indifference than like freedom.

NEEDING AND GIVING, LOVING AND HAVING

C. S. Lewis has divided love into these two kinds: "need-love" and "gift-love." Abraham Maslow also divides love into two kinds. The first he calls "deficiency-love" and the second he calls "being-love." The distinction is significant and has to be understood.

The "need-love" or the "deficiency-love" depends on the

other; it is immature love. In fact it is not truly love—it is a need. You use the other, you use the other as a means. You exploit, you manipulate, you dominate. But the other is reduced, the other is almost destroyed. And exactly the same is being done by the other. He is trying to manipulate you, to dominate you, to possess you, to use you. To use another human being is very unloving. So it only appears like love; it is a false coin. But this is what happens to almost ninety-nine percent of people because the first lesson of love that you learn is in your childhood.

A child is born, he depends on the mother. His love toward the mother is a "deficiency-love"—he needs the mother, he cannot survive without the mother. He loves the mother because mother is his life. In fact it is not really love—he will love any woman, whosoever will protect him, whosoever will help him to survive, whosoever will fill up his need. The mother is a sort of food that he eats. It is not only milk that he gets from the mother, it is love also—and that too is a need. Millions of people remain childish all their lives; they never grow up. They grow in age but they never grow in their minds; their psychology

> Interdependence happens very rarely, but whenever it happens a part of paradise falls on the earth. Two persons, neither independent nor dependent but in a tremendous synchronicity, as if breathing for each other, one soul in two bodies—whenever that happens, love has happened.

remains juvenile, immature. They are always needing love, they are hankering for it like food.

Man becomes mature the moment he starts loving rather than needing. He starts overflowing, sharing; he starts giving. The emphasis is totally different. With the first, the emphasis is on how to get more. With the second, the emphasis is on how to give, how to give more, and how to give unconditionally. This is growth, maturity, coming to you. A mature person gives. Only a mature person can give, because only a mature person has it. Then love is not dependent. Then you can be loving whether the other is or is not. Then love is not a relationship, it is a state.

> Millions of people remain childish all their lives; they never grow up. They grow in age but they never grow in their minds; their psychology remains juvenile, immature. They are always needing love, they are hankering for it like food.

What happens when a flower blooms in a deep forest with nobody to appreciate it, nobody to know its fragrance, nobody to pass by and say "beautiful," nobody to taste its beauty, its joy, nobody to share— what happens to the flower? It dies? It suffers? It becomes panicky? It commits suicide? It goes on blooming, it simply goes on blooming. It does not make any difference whether somebody passes by or not; it is irrelevant. It goes on spreading its fragrance to the winds. It goes on offering its joy to God, to the whole. If I am alone, then too I will be as loving as when I am with you. It is not you who are creating my love. If you were creating my love, then naturally, when you are gone my love will be gone. You are not pulling my love out, I am showering it on you—this is "gift-love," it is "being-love."

And I don't really agree with C. S. Lewis and Abraham Maslow. The first love that they call "love" is not love, it is a need. How can a need be love? Love is a luxury. It is abundance. It is having so much life that you don't know what to do with it, so you share. It is having so many songs in your heart that you have to sing them—whether anybody listens is not relevant. If nobody listens then also you will have to sing your song, you will have to dance your dance. The other can have it, the other can miss it—but as far as you are concerned it is flowing; it is overflowing. Rivers don't flow for you; they are flowing whether you are there or not. They don't flow for your thirst, they don't flow for your thirsty fields; they are simply flowing there. You can quench your thirst, you can miss—that's up to you. The river was not really flowing for you, the river was just flowing. It is accidental that you can get the water for your field, it is accidental that you can get water for your needs.

> Man becomes mature the moment he starts loving rather than needing. He starts overflowing, sharing, he starts giving. The emphasis is totally different. With the first, the emphasis is on how to get more. With the second, the emphasis is on how to give, how to give more, and how to give unconditionally.

When you depend on the other there is always misery. The moment you depend, you start feeling miserable because dependence is slavery. Then you start taking revenge in subtle ways, because the person you have to depend upon becomes powerful over you. Nobody likes anybody to be powerful over them, nobody likes to be dependent because dependence kills freedom. And love cannot flower in dependence—love is a flower of freedom; it needs space, it needs absolute space. The other has not to interfere with it. It is very delicate.

> How can a need be love? Love is a luxury. It is abundance. It is having so much life that you don't know what to do with it, so you share. It is having so many songs in your heart that you have to sing them—whether anybody listens or not is irrelevant.

When you are dependent the other will certainly dominate you, and you will try to dominate the other. That's the fight that goes on between so-called lovers. They are intimate enemies, continually fighting. Husbands and wives—what are they doing? Loving is very rare; fighting is the rule, loving is an exception. And in every way they try to dominate—even through love they try to dominate. If the husband asks the wife, the wife refuses, she is reluctant. She is very miserly: she gives but very reluctantly, she wants you to wag your tail around her. And so is the case with the husband. When the wife is in need and asks him, the husband says that he is tired. In the office there was too much work, he is really overworked, and he would like to go to sleep.

These are ways to manipulate, to starve the other, to make him more and more hungry so that he becomes more and more dependent. Naturally, women are more diplomatic about it than men because the man is already powerful. He need not find subtle and cunning ways to be powerful, he is powerful. He manages the money—that is his power. Muscularly, he is stronger. Down the centuries he has conditioned the mind of the woman that he is more powerful and she is not powerful. The man has always tried to find a woman who is in every way lesser than him. A man does not want to be married to a woman who is more educated than him, because then the power is at stake. He does not want to marry a woman who is taller than him, because a taller woman looks superior. He does not want to marry a woman who is too much of an intellectual, because then she argues, and argument can destroy power. A man does not want a woman who is very famous, because then he becomes secondary. And down the centuries man has asked for a woman who is younger than him. Why can't the wife be older than you? What is wrong? But an older woman is more experienced—that destroys power.

So man has always asked for a lesser woman—that's why women have lost their height. There is no reason for them to be of lesser height than men, no reason at all; they have lost their height because only the smaller woman was always chosen. By and by the thing has entered in their minds so deeply that they have lost their height. They have lost intelligence because an intelligent woman was not needed; an intelligent woman was a freak. You will be surprised to know that just in this century their height is increasing again. Even their bones are becoming bigger, the skeleton is becoming bigger. Just within fifty years . . . particularly in America. And their brains are also growing and becoming bigger than they used to be, the skull is becoming bigger.

> When you don't have love, you ask the other to give it to you; you are a beggar. And the other is asking you to give it to him or to her. Now, two beggars spreading their hands before each other, and both are hoping that the other has it... Naturally both feel defeated finally, and both feel cheated.

With the idea of freedom for women, some deep conditioning has been destroyed. Man already had power so he did not need to be very clever, did not need to be very indirect. Women didn't have power. When you don't have power you have to be more diplomatic—that is a substitute. The only way they could feel powerful is that they were needed, that the man was continuously in need of them. This is not love, this is a bargain, and they are continuously haggling over the price. It is a constant struggle.

C. S. Lewis and Abraham Maslow divide love in two. I don't divide in two. I say that the first kind of love is just a name, a false coin; it is not true. Only the second kind of love is love.

Love happens only when you are mature. You become capable of loving only when you are a grown-up. When you know that love is not a need but an overflow—"being-love" or "gift-love"—then you give without any conditions.

The first kind, the so-called love, derives from a person's deep need for another, while "gift-love" or "being-love" overflows from one mature person to another out of abundance. One is flooded with it. You have it and it starts moving around you, just as when you light a lamp, the rays start spreading into the darkness. Love is a by-product of being. When you *are*, you have the aura of love around you. When you are not, you don't have that aura around you. And when you don't have that aura around you, you ask the other to give love to you. Let it be repeated: when you don't have love, you ask the other to give it to you; you are a beggar. And the other is asking you to give it to him or to her. Now, two beggars spreading their hands before each other, and both are hoping that the other has it . . . Naturally both feel defeated finally, and both feel cheated.

You can ask any husband and any wife, you can ask any lovers—they both feel cheated. It was your projection that the other had it—if you have a wrong projection, what can the other do about it? Your projection has been broken; the other did not prove according to your projection, that's all. But the other has no obligation to prove himself according to your expectations.

And you have cheated the other—that is the feeling of the other, because the other was hoping that love would be flowing from you. You both were hoping love would be flowing from the other, and both were empty—how can love happen? At the most you can be miserable together. Before, you used to be miserable alone, separate; now you can be miserable together. And remember, whenever two persons are miserable together it is not a simple addition, it is a multiplication.

Alone you were feeling frustrated, now together you feel frustrated. One thing is good about it, in that now you can throw the responsibility on the other—the other is making you miserable, that is the good point. You can feel at ease. "Nothing is wrong with me, but the other . . . What to do with such a wife—nasty, nagging? One has to be miserable. What to do with such a husband—ugly, a miser?" Now you can throw the responsibility on the other; you have found a scapegoat. But misery remains, becomes multiplied.

Now this is the paradox: those who fall in love don't have any love, that's why they fall in love. And because they don't have any love, they cannot give. And one thing more—an immature person always falls in love with another immature person, because only they can understand each other's language. A mature person loves a mature person. An immature person loves an immature person.

You can go on changing your husband or your wife a thousand and one times, you will again find the same type of woman and the same misery repeated—in different forms, but the same misery repeated, it is almost the same. You can change your wife, but you are not changed—now who is going to choose the new wife? You will choose. The choice will come out of your immaturity again. You will choose a similar type of woman again.

The basic problem of love is to first become mature. Then you will find a mature partner; then immature people will not attract you at all. It is just like that. If you are twenty-five years of age, you don't fall in love with a baby two years old. Exactly like that, when you are a mature person psychologically, spiritually, you don't fall in love with a baby. It does not happen. It *cannot* happen, you can see that it is going to be meaningless.

In fact a mature person does not fall in love, he rises in love. The word *fall* is not right. Only immature people fall; they stumble and fall down in love. Somehow they were managing and standing. Now they cannot manage and they cannot stand—they find a woman and they are gone, they find a man and they are gone. They were always ready to fall on the ground and to creep. They don't have the backbone, the spine; they don't have the integrity to stand alone.

A mature person has the integrity to be alone. And when a mature person gives love, he gives without any strings attached to it—he simply gives. When a mature person gives love, he feels grateful that you have accepted his love, not vice versa. He does not expect you to be thankful for it—no, not at all, he does not even need your thanks. He thanks you for accepting his love. And when two mature persons are in love, one of the greatest paradoxes of life happens, one of the most beautiful phenomena: they are together and yet tremendously alone. They are together so much so that they are almost one, but their oneness does not destroy their individuality—in fact, it enhances it, they become more individual. Two mature persons in love help each other to become more free. There is no politics involved, no diplomacy, no effort to dominate.

> The basic problem of love is to first become mature. Then you will find a mature partner, then immature people will not attract you at all. It is just like that.

How can you dominate the person you love? Just think it

over—domination is a sort of hatred, anger, enmity. How can you think of dominating a person you love? You would love to see the person totally free, independent; you will give him more individuality. That's why I call it the greatest paradox: they are together so much that they are almost one, but still in that oneness they are individuals. Their individualities are not effaced—they have become enhanced. The other has enriched them as far as their freedom is concerned.

Immature people falling in love destroy each other's freedom, create a bondage, make a prison. Mature persons in love help each other to be free; they help each other to destroy all sorts of bondages. And when love flows with freedom there is beauty. When love flows with dependence there is ugliness.

Remember, freedom is a higher value than love. That's why in India, the ultimate we call moksha; moksha means "freedom." Freedom is a higher value than love. So if love is destroying freedom, it is not of worth. Love can be dropped, freedom has to be saved—freedom is a higher value. And without freedom you can never be happy, it is not possible. Freedom is the intrinsic desire of each man, each

> When two mature persons are in love, one of the greatest paradoxes of life happens, one of the most beautiful phenomena: they are together and yet tremendously alone. They are together so much so that they are almost one, but their oneness does not destroy their individuality.

woman—utter freedom, absolute freedom. So anything that becomes destructive to freedom, one starts hating it.

Don't you hate the man you love? Don't you hate the woman you love? You hate! It is a necessary evil, you have to tolerate it. Because you cannot be alone you have to manage to be with somebody, and you have to adjust to the other's demands. You have to tolerate, you have to bear them.

Love, to be really love, has to be "being-love," "gift-love." "Being-love" means a state of love—when you have arrived home, when you have known who you are, then love arises in your being. Then the fragrance spreads and you can give it to others. How can you give something that you don't have? To give it, the first basic requirement is to have it.

LOVE AND MARRIAGE

My suggestion is that marriage should happen after the honeymoon, never before it. Only if everything goes right, only then marriage should happen.

Honeymoon after marriage is very dangerous. As far as I know, ninety-nine percent of marriages are finished by the time the honeymoon is finished. But then you are caught, then you have no way to escape. Then the whole society—the law, the court, everybody—is against you if you leave the wife or the wife leaves you. Then the whole morality, the religion, the priest, everybody is against you.

In fact society should create all barriers possible for marriage and no barrier for divorce. Society should not allow people to marry so easily. The court should create barriers—live with the woman for two years at least, then the court can allow you to get married. Right now they are doing just the reverse. If you want to get married, nobody asks whether you are ready or whether it is just a whim, just because you like the nose of the woman. What foolishness! One cannot live with just a beautiful nose. After two days the nose will be forgotten—who looks at one's own wife's nose? The wife never looks beautiful, the husband never looks beautiful; once you are acquainted, beauty disappears.

Two persons should be allowed to live together long enough to become acquainted, familiar with each other. Before that, even if they want to get married they should not be allowed. Then divorces will disappear from the world. The divorces exist because marriages are wrong and forced. The divorces exist because marriages are done in a romantic mood.

> Two persons should be allowed to live together long enough to become acquainted, familiar with each other. Before that, even if they want to get married they should not be allowed. Then divorces will disappear from the world.

A romantic mood is good if you are a poet—and poets are not known to be good husbands or good wives. In fact poets are almost always bachelors; they fool around but they never get caught, and hence their romance remains alive. They go on writing poetry, beautiful poetry. . . . One should not get married to a woman or to a man in a poetic mood. Let the prose mood come, then settle. Because the day-to-day life is more like prose than like poetry.

One should become mature enough. Maturity means that one is no longer a romantic fool. One understands life, one understands the responsibility of life, one understands the problems of being together with a person. One accepts all those difficulties and yet decides to live with the person. One is not hoping that there is only going to be heaven, all roses. One is not hoping nonsense; one knows reality is tough, it is rough. There are roses but far and few in between; there are many thorns.

When you have become alert to all of these problems and still you decide that it is worthwhile to risk and be with a person rather than to be alone, then get married. Then marriages will never kill love, because this love is realistic. Marriage can kill only romantic love. And romantic love is what people call puppy love. One should not depend on it. One should not think about it as nourishment. It may be just like ice cream—you can eat it sometimes, but don't depend on it. Life has to be more realistic, more prose.

And marriage itself never destroys anything. Marriage simply brings out whatsoever is hidden in you—it brings it out. If love is hidden inside you, marriage brings it out. If love was just a preten-

> One should not get married to a woman or to a man in a poetic mood. Let the prose mood come, then settle. Because the day-to-day life is more like prose than like poetry.

sion, just a bait, then sooner or later it has to disappear. And then your reality, your ugly personality comes up. Marriage simply is an opportunity, so whatsoever you had within you will come out.

Love is not destroyed by marriage. Love is destroyed by people who don't know how to love. Love is destroyed because in the first place love is not; you have been living in a dream. Reality destroys that dream. Otherwise love is something eternal, part of eternity. If you grow, if you know the art and you accept the realities of love life, then it goes on growing every day. Marriage becomes a tremendous opportunity to grow into love.

> Love is something eternal, part of eternity. If you grow, if you know the art and you accept the realities of love life, then it goes on growing every day. Marriage becomes a tremendous opportunity to grow into love.

Nothing can destroy love. If it is there, it goes on growing. But my feeling is that in most cases it is not there in the first place. You misunderstood yourself, something else was there—maybe sex was there, sex appeal was there. Then it is going to be destroyed because once you have made love to a woman then the sex appeal disappears. Sex appeal is only with the unknown—once you have tasted the body of the woman or the man, then the sex appeal disappears. If your love was only sex appeal, then it is bound to disappear.

So never misunderstand love for something else. If love is really

love. . . . What do I mean when I say "really lo
just being in the presence of the other you fee
just being together you feel ecstatic, just the v
other fulfills something deep in your
heart . . . something starts singing in
your heart, you fall into harmony.
Just the very presence of the other
helps you to be together; you become more individual, more centered, more grounded. Then it is
love.

Love is not a passion, love is not
an emotion. Love is a very deep understanding that somebody somehow
completes you. Somebody makes
you a full circle. The presence of the
other enhances your presence. Love
gives freedom to be yourself; it is not
possessiveness.

So watch—never think of sex as
love, otherwise you will be deceived.
Be alert, and when you start feeling
with someone that just the presence,
the pure presence—nothing else,
nothing else is needed; you don't ask
anything, just the presence, just that

> Love is not a passion,
> love is not an
> emotion. Love is a
> very deep
> understanding that
> somebody somehow
> completes you.
> Somebody makes you
> a full circle. The
> presence of the other
> enhances your
> presence. Love gives
> freedom to be
> yourself; it is not
> possessiveness.

the other is, is enough to make you happy . . . Something starts
flowering within you, a thousand and one lotuses bloom, then
you are in love. And then you can pass through all the difficulties

.t reality creates. Many anguishes, many anxieties—you will be able to pass through all of them and your love will be flowering more and more, because all those situations will become challenges. And your love, by overcoming them, will grow more and more strong.

Love is eternity. If it is there, then it goes on growing and growing. Love knows the beginning but does not know the end.

PARENT AND CHILD

A child can be born not only through biological sexual intercourse but also through a deep meditative love. Meditative love means melting into each other's beings, not just the bodies. It means putting your egos, your religions, your ideologies aside—becoming simple and innocent. If a child is conceived by such parents, then the child will not be conditioned at all.

There are a few things that you have to understand—I cannot give any proofs for them, they are beyond proofs. Only your experience will give you the proof.

For example, the biological organism is capable of transcending itself. It transcends in certain moments. Those are the moments most cherished in the human mind, because in those moments you have known freedom, an expanded self, an utter silence and peace; love without its counterpart, hate, following it. That moment we call orgasm. Biology gives you orgasm; that is the most precious gift from blind biology. You can use those moments of freedom, melting, disappearing, for meditation. There is no better space from which to jump into meditation than orgasm. Two lovers feeling one soul in two bodies . . . everything has stopped for the moment, even time has stopped. There are no thoughts, the mind has stopped. You are in your simple isness. Those are the little spaces from where you can get beyond biology.

All that you have to know is that this is what meditation is: timelessness, egolessness, silence, blissfulness, an all-pervading joy, overwhelming ecstasy.

This has happened through biology between two persons. Once you know that it can happen in your aloneness too, you just have to fulfill those conditions. My own understanding is that man came to know about meditation through sexual orgasm, because in life there is no other moment that comes so close to meditativeness.

But all the religions are against sex. They are for meditation but they are not for the beginning, the basic experience that will lead you to meditation. So they have created a poor humanity—not only materially poor but spiritually poor too. They have conditioned your mind against sex so much that under biological pressure you go into it, but in that pressure you cannot experience the orgasmic freedom, the infinity that suddenly becomes available to you—the eternity in the moment, the depth, the abysmal depth of the experience.

Because man has been deprived of orgasmic blissfulness he has

> My own understanding is that man came to know about meditation through sexual orgasm, because in life there is no other moment which comes so close to meditativeness.

become incapable of knowing what meditation is. And that's what all the religions want, that you never become meditative—talk about it, read about it, do research on it, listen to lectures on it. . . . All that will create more frustration in you because you understand everything about meditation intellectually, but you don't have any existential base, not even a drop of the experience that can prove that if the drop is there, the ocean also must be somewhere.

> Biology is your nature, it has nothing but compassion for you. It has given you everything possible that is needed to go higher, to reach to a supernatural state.

The drop is the existential proof of the ocean. Biology is far more compassionate than your churches, synagogues, temples, and mosques. Although biology is blind, it is not so blind as your Moses, Krishna, Jesus, Mohammed. Biology is your nature, it has nothing but compassion for you. It has given you everything possible that is needed to go higher, to reach to a supernatural state.

My whole life I have been fighting against idiots. They cannot answer me, my argument, which is simple: you talk about meditation but you will have to give some existential proof in human life; otherwise, people will understand only words. You will have to give them something that can make them aware of what is possible—love made without any guilt, without any hurry, without thinking that you are doing something wrong. You will be doing the best and the most right thing in the world.

It is strange to see that people can kill without any guilt—not one but millions of people—but they cannot create a child without guilt. All the religions have been nothing but a calamity. Make love only when you are ready to be in a meditative space. And create a meditative atmosphere while you are making love. You should treat the place as sacred. Creating life . . . what can be more sacred? Do it as beautifully, as aesthetically, as joyously as possible. There should be no hurry. And if the two lovers meet in such an atmosphere outside, and such a silent space within, they will attract a soul who is the highest available.

You give birth to a child according to your state of love. If a parent is disappointed he should think about it, that this is the child he deserved. The parents never created a possibility for a higher and more evolved soul to enter into the womb—because the male sperm and the female egg only create an opportunity for a soul to enter. They create the opportunity for a body so that some soul can become embodied. But you will attract only that kind of person that your sexual activity makes possible.

If the world is full of idiots and mediocre people, you are responsible—I mean, parents are responsible. They never thought

> Make love only when you are ready to be in a meditative space. And create a meditative atmosphere while you are making love. You should treat the place as sacred. Creating life . . . what can be more sacred? Do it as beautifully, as aesthetically, as joyously as possible.

about it, their children are accidental. There cannot be a bigger crime than to create a life accidentally.

Prepare for it. And the most essential thing is to understand the orgasmic moment: thoughtless, timeless, mindless, just a pure awareness. In that pure awareness you can attract a Gautam Buddha. The way you are making love, it is strange that more Adolf Hitlers, Mussolinis, Stalins, Nadirshahs, Tamerlanes, Genghis Khans are not attracted. You attract only mediocre people. You don't attract the lowest either, because for the lowest your love has to be almost a rape. For the highest, your love has to be a meditation.

The child's life begins from the moment the soul enters into the womb. If it has come into a meditative space, it is possible to have a child without conditioning him. In fact, a child who is born out of meditation cannot be conditioned; he will rebel against it. Only mediocre people can be conditioned.

And a couple who is capable of meditativeness while making love is no ordinary couple. They will be respectful to the child. The child is a guest from the unknown, and you have to be respectful to the guest. Parents who are not respectful to their children are bound to destroy their lives. Your respect, your love, your gratitude that, "You have chosen us as your parents," will be responded to with deeper respect, more gratitude, more love.

And when you love a person, you cannot condition him. When you love a person, you give him freedom, you give him protection. When you love a person, you would not like him to be just a carbon copy of yourself, you would like him to be a unique individual. And to make him unique you will arrange all the conditions, all the challenges that provoke his potential.

You will not burden him with knowledgeability, because you

would like him to know the truth himself. <u>Any borrowed truth is a lie</u>. <u>Unless it is experienced by you, it is never the truth.</u>

You will help the child to experience more and more things. You will not tell him lies, that there is a God—it is a lie, because you have not seen God. Your parents lied to you and you are repeating it in your turn to your child. Your parents conditioned you, and what is your life? A long misery from cradle to grave. Do you want your child's life also to be just a misery, full of suffering, anxiety, despair?

There is only one statement in the whole Holy Bible that I am not against. The statement is, "God can forgive everything, but not despair." Whoever wrote it must have been a man of immense understanding. God cannot forgive only one thing, and that is despair. But everybody is living in despair—God or no God, despair is a reality. It is self-destruction. If you love your child, you will help him rejoice, laugh, enjoy, dance. But just the opposite is being done.

> The child is a guest from the unknown, and you have to be respectful to the guest. Parents who are not respectful to their children are bound to destroy their lives. Your respect, your love, your gratitude that, "You have chosen us as your parents," will be responded to with deeper respect, more gratitude, more love.

In my house in my childhood, it used to be that when some guest was coming they used to get rid of me by sending me somewhere. And the moment they started talking about sending me somewhere—that I have to go to see the doctor because I have had a cold for so many days, I would say, "Nothing doing. I know my cold and I know the doctor; I will choose my time to go. At least this time I cannot go—cold or cancer, it makes no difference."

They said, "But why?"

I said, "I know somebody is coming to the house, and you are afraid." And they were naturally afraid, because I made them feel embarrassed. The guest may be some important person, and I may do something that will spoil their whole relationship.

Once, eating, suddenly I started laughing. The whole family knew that something was bound to happen, because there was a guest. But the guest was shocked. He said, "Why are you laughing?"

I said, "Laughing needs no cause. In fact, I should ask you, 'Why are you all sitting with long faces?' Laughter has an intrinsic value; long faces don't have any value at all. And since you have come, even people in my family are looking very sad, serious. I don't understand what is wrong with you. Do you create this kind of atmosphere wherever you go?"

I may suddenly start dancing. The conversation between the guest and my parents would stop suddenly, because I was dancing in the middle of them. They would say, "You can go out and play."

I said, "I know the exact spot where to dance. If you choose to go out, you can go and have your stupid conversation—which means nothing! Talking about the weather and the season . . . you all know, even I know. What is the point?"

In polite conversation people never discuss subjects that are controversial because that may create some antagonism. They discuss only noncontroversial subjects—the weather. . . . Naturally, there is no controversy about it. If it is cold, it is cold; if it is hot, it is hot.

"And I am dancing here only to make you realize that you are wasting your time. Better join me in the dance!"

A child who is not conditioned is in many ways embarrassing to the parents. But if they love, they will be ready to do anything. Even if it brings embarrassment, there is no harm. Their child is growing into a unique being. They will help him to remain free, to remain open, to remain available to the unknown future.

They will help him be a seeker, not a believer. They will not make him a Christian, or a Jew, or a Hindu, or a Mohammedan, because all these religions have done so much harm—it is more than enough. It is time for all the religions to disappear from the planet. Unconditioned children can make that miracle happen because tomorrow they will be young people, mature, and they will not be Christians and Hindus and Mohammedans. They will be just seekers; seeking will be their religion. That's my definition of a sannyasin: searching, seeking, inquiring is his religion. Beliefs stop all inquiry.

Share with the child all your experiences. Make him aware that he was conceived in a very loving orgasmic moment, that love is a great gift of existence. And you have to make love the central point of your life, because only through love can you step beyond blind nature into the world of supernature where no blindness exists, where you become a seer.

Yes, it is possible to have an unconditioned and free child, but not possible through biology alone. It is possible if you are courageous enough to make your love your temple, your place of meditation. Then you will be attracting a soul already having the potential of uniqueness. And then give him every possibility for freedom, even if it goes against you. The freedom of your child is more valuable, because your child is the future of mankind.

Your days are past—what does it matter if the future goes against you? What have you gained by the past? You are empty, you are beggars. Do you want your children also to be empty and beggars? That's what every parent is trying to do—to reproduce copies, carbon copies. And remember, existence accepts only the originals. Carbon copies are not acceptable in existence.

Let your child have his original face.

It may create fear in you, it may create concern in you, but those are your problems. Don't in any way inhibit the child. And a child who has been given freedom—even against his own parents—will respect you forever, will remain grateful to you forever. Right now, just the opposite is the case: every child is full of anger, rage, hatred for the parents, because what they have done to him is unforgivable.

> Your days are past—what does it matter if the future goes against you? What have you gained by the past? You are empty, you are beggars. Do you want your children also to be empty and beggars? That's what every parent is trying to do—to reproduce copies, carbon copies. And remember, existence accepts only the originals.

74

So by giving freedom, by allowing the child to be himself whatever that means, accepting him in his natural self wherever it leads, you are creating a child who will love and respect you. You have been not only ordinary fathers and mothers, you have been givers of life, freedom, uniqueness. He will carry the beautiful memory in his heart forever, and his gratitude toward you will make him absolutely certain that what has been done for him, he has to do for the future generations.

If every generation behaves toward children with love and respect, and gives them freedom to grow, all this nonsense of the generation gap will disappear. If you respect your children, if you are friends to your children, no generation gap is possible.

IT IS ALWAYS GOOD TO COME TO AN UNDERSTANDING WITH THE PARENTS. It is one of the basic things. Gurdjieff used to say, "Unless you are in good communion with your parents, you have missed your life." Because it is something very deep-rooted. . . . If some anger persists between you and your parents, you will never feel at ease. Wherever you are, you will feel a little guilty. You will never be able to forget it and forgive it. Parents are not just a social relationship. It is out of them that you have come— you are part of them, a branch of their tree. You are still rooted in them.

When the parents die, something very deep-rooted dies within you. When parents die, for the first time you feel alone, uprooted. So while they are alive, everything that can be done should be done so that an understanding can arise and you can communicate with them and they can communicate with you. Then things settle and the accounts are closed. Then when they leave the world—they will leave someday—you will not feel guilty, you will not repent; you will know that things have settled. They have been happy with you; you have been happy with them.

> If every generation behaves toward children with love and respect, and gives them freedom to grow, all this nonsense of the generation gap will disappear. If you respect your children, if you are friends to your children, no generation gap is possible.

The love relationship starts with the parents and it also ends with them. It comes to a full circle. If somewhere the circle is broken, your whole being will remain uneasy. One feels tremendously happy when one can communicate with one's own parents. That is the most difficult thing in the world to do because the gap is so big. The parents never think that you are grown up so they never directly communicate with you. They simply order you: "Do this" or "Don't do that." They never take account of your freedom and your spirit, your being . . . no respect. They take it for granted that you have listened to them.

A child feels very annoyed from the very beginning, because whenever the parent says "Do this" or "Don't do that," he feels that his freedom is being cut. He is being repressed. He resists, resents, and that resistance continues like a wound. The gap becomes bigger and bigger. It has to be bridged. If you can bridge your relationship with your mother, suddenly you will feel that the whole earth is bridged. You are more rooted in the earth. If you can bridge your relationship with your father, you are at home with the sky. They are symbolic, representatives of the earth and the sky. And man is like a tree, which needs both the earth and the sky.

LOVE PLUS AWARENESS EQUALS BEING

Love is a must for spiritual growth. And moreover, love functions as a mirror. It is very difficult to know yourself unless you have looked at your face in the eyes of someone who loves you. Just as you have to look into the mirror to see your physical face, you have to look in the mirror of love to see your spiritual face. Love is a spiritual mirror. It nourishes you, it integrates you, it makes you ready for the inner journey, it reminds you of your original face.

In moments of deep love there are glimpses of the original face, although those glimpses are coming as reflections. Just as on a full moon night you see the moon reflected in the lake, in the silent

> The love relationship starts with the parents and it also ends with them. It comes to a full circle. If somewhere the circle is broken, your whole being will remain uneasy. One feels tremendously happy when one can communicate with one's own parents. That is the most difficult thing in the world to do because the gap is so big.

lake, so love functions as a lake. The moon reflected in the lake is the beginning of the search for the real moon. If you have never seen the moon reflected in the lake you may never search for the real moon. You will go again and again into the lake to search for the moon because in the beginning you will think this is where the real moon is, somewhere deep down at the bottom of the lake. You will dive again and again and you will come up empty-handed; you will not find the moon there.

Then one day it will dawn on you that maybe this moon is just a reflection. That is a great insight—then you can look upward. Then where is the moon if this is a reflection? If it is a reflection you have to look in the opposite direction. The reflection was there, deep in the lake—the real must be somewhere above the lake. For the first time you look upward, and the journey has started.

Love gives you glimpses of meditation, reflections of the moon in the lake—although they are reflections, not the moon itself. So love can never satisfy you. In fact, love will make you more and more dissatisfied, discontented. Love will make you more and more aware of what is possible, but it will not deliver the goods. It will frustrate you—and only in deep frustration lies the possibility of turning back to your own being. Only lovers know the joy of meditation. Those who have never loved and have never been frustrated in love, those who have never dived into the lake of love in search of the moon and are never frustrated, will never look up to the real moon in the sky. They will never become aware of it.

The person who loves is bound to become religious sooner or later. But the person who does not love—the politician, for example, who cannot love any person, he loves only power— will never become religious. Or the person who is obsessed with money—who loves only money, who knows only one love, the love of money—will never become religious. It will be very difficult for him for so many reasons. Money can be possessed; you can have money and you can possess it. It is easy to possess money, it is difficult to possess a beloved—impossible, in fact. You will try to possess, but how can you possess a living person? The living person will resist in every way, will fight to the last. Nobody wants to lose their freedom.

Love is not as valuable as freedom is. Love is a great value, but not higher than freedom. So one would like to be loving but one would not like to be imprisoned by love. Hence, sooner or later you become frustrated. You try to possess, and the more you try to possess the more impossible love becomes and the more the other starts going away from you. The less you possess, the closer you feel to the other. If you don't possess at all, if there is freedom flowing between the lovers, there is great love.

> Love will make you more and more aware of what is possible, but it will not deliver the goods. It will frustrate you—and only in deep frustration lies the possibility of turning back to your own being. Only lovers know the joy of meditation.

First, the effort to possess a person is bound to fail. In that frustration you will be thrown back on yourself. Second, if you have learned not to possess the person, if you have learned that freedom is a higher value than love, a far superior value to love, then sooner or later you will see that freedom will bring you to yourself, freedom will become your awareness, meditation.

Freedom is another aspect of meditation. Either start with freedom and you will become aware, or start with awareness and you will become free. They go together. Love is a kind of subtle bondage, but it is an essential experience, very essential for maturity.

There is a beautiful definition of realness through love in Margery Williams's beautiful book *The Velveteen Rabbit*.

"What is REAL?" asked the Rabbit one day. "Does it mean having things that buzz inside of you and a stick-out handle?"

"Real isn't how you are made," said the Skin Horse. "It's a thing that happens to you. When a child loves you for a long, long time, not just to play with, but REALLY loves you, then you become Real."

"Does it hurt?" asked the Rabbit.

"Sometimes," said the Skin Horse, for he was always truthful. "When you are Real you don't mind being hurt."

"Does it happen all at once, like being wound up," he asked, "or bit by bit?"

"It doesn't happen all at once," said the Skin Horse. "You become. It takes a long time. That's why it doesn't often happen to people who break easily, or have sharp edges, or who have to be carefully kept. Generally, by the time you are Real, most of your hair has been loved off, and your eyes drop out and you get loose in the joints and very shabby. But these things don't matter at all, because once you are Real you can't be ugly, except to people who don't understand . . . once you are Real, you can't become unreal again. It lasts for always."

Love makes you real; otherwise you remain just a fantasy, a dream with no substance in it. Love gives you substance, love gives you integrity, loves makes you centered. But it is only half of the journey; the other half has to be completed in meditation, in awareness. But love prepares you for the other half. Love is the beginning half and awareness is the ending half. Between these two you attain to God. Between love and awareness, between these two banks, the river of being flows.

> Freedom is another aspect of meditation. Either start with freedom and you will become aware, or start with awareness and you will become free. They go together. Love is a kind of subtle bondage—they go together—but it is an essential experience, very essential for maturity.

Don't avoid love. Go through it, with all its pains. Yes, it hurts, but if you are in love it doesn't matter. In fact, all those hurts strengthen you. Sometimes it really hurts badly, terribly, but all those wounds are necessary to provoke you, to challenge you, to make you less sleepy. All those dangerous situations are necessary to make you alert. Love prepares the ground, and in the soil of love the seed of meditation can grow—and only in the soil of love.

So those who escape from the world out of fear will never attain to meditation. They can sit in the Himalayan caves for lives together, they will not attain to meditation. It is not possible—they have not earned it. First it has to be earned in the world; first they have to prepare the soil. And it is only love that prepares the soil.

Hence my insistence not to renounce the world. Be in it, take its challenge, accept its dangers, its hurts, wounds. Go through it. Don't avoid it, don't try to find a shortcut because there is none. It is a struggle, it is arduous, it is an uphill task, but that is how one reaches the peak.

And the joy will be more, far more than if you were dropped on the peak by a helicopter, because then you will have reached there ungrown; you will not be able to enjoy it. Just think of the difference. You try hard to reach Everest. It is so dangerous—every possibility of dying on the way, every possibility of never reaching to the peak; hazardous, dangerous. Death is waiting for you at each step, so many traps and so many possibilities of being defeated rather than being successful. Out of one hundred possibilities there is only one possibility that you may reach. But the closer you come to the peak, the higher the joy rises in you. Your spirit soars high. You earn it, it is not free. And the more you have paid for it, the more you will enjoy it. Then imagine—you can be dropped from a helicopter on the top. You will stand on the top and you will just look silly, stupid—what are you doing here? Within five minutes you will be finished, you will say, "So I have seen it! There is nothing much here!"

The journey creates the goal. The goal is not sitting there at the end of the journey, the journey creates it at each step. The journey is the goal. The journey and the goal are not separate, they are not two things. The end and the means are not two things. The end is spread over all the way; all the means contain the end in them.

So never miss any opportunity of living, of being alive, of being responsible, of being committed, of getting involved. Don't be a coward. Face life, encounter it. And then slowly, slowly something inside you will crystallize.

Yes, it takes time. The Skin Horse is right: "Generally, by the time you are Real, most of your hair has been loved off, and your eyes drop out and you get loose in the joints and very shabby. But these things don't matter at all, because once you are Real you can't be ugly except to people who don't understand . . . once you are Real, you can't become unreal again. It lasts for always." It is forever.

But one has to earn it. Let me repeat it: in life you cannot get anything free. And if you do get it, it is useless. You have to pay, and the more you pay for it the more you will get out of it. If you can risk your whole life in love, great will be your attainment. Love will send you back to yourself; it will give you a few reflections of meditation. The first glimpses of meditation happen in love. And then a great desire arises in you to attain to those glimpses, not only as glimpses but as states, so that you can live in those states forever and forever. Love gives you the taste of meditation.

A loving, orgasmic experience is the first experience of samadhi, of ecstasy. It will make you more thirsty. Now you will know what is possible and now you cannot be satisfied with the mundane. The sacred has penetrated you, the sacred has reached your heart. God has touched your heart, you have felt that touch. Now you would like to live in that moment forever, you would like that moment to become your whole life. It does become—and unless it becomes, man remains discontented.

Love on the one hand will give you great joy and on the other hand will give you a thirst for eternal joy.

> A loving, orgasmic experience is the first experience of samadhi, of ecstasy. It will make you more thirsty. Now you will know what is possible and now you cannot be satisfied with the mundane. The sacred has penetrated you, the sacred has reached your heart.

STANDING AT THE CROSSROADS

※

WHEN ETERNITY PENETRATES TIME

Time is that in which we live—it is horizontal. It is from A to B to C to D; it is in a line. Eternity is vertical. It is not from A to B and from B to C. It is from A to more A to still more A. It goes on upward. The moment is rare when eternity penetrates time, because it happens only when meditation has reached ripening, maturity, when you have touched your innermost core.

Then suddenly you become aware that you are a crossroads. One line goes horizontal—in other words, mediocre, ordinary, meaningless, and leading finally to death. The horizontal line is continuously moving toward the graveyard.

I have told you the story, significant in many ways:

A great king in his dreams saw a shadow, and became afraid even in the dream. He asked the shadow, "What do you want?"

The shadow said, "I have not come to ask for anything. I have come just to inform you that this evening at the right place, when the sun is setting, you will breathe your last breath. Ordinarily I don't come to inform people, but you are a great emperor; it is just to pay respect to you."

The emperor became so afraid that he woke up perspiring, could not think what to do. The only thing he could think of was to call all the wise men, astrologers, prophets, and to find out the meaning of the dream. Dream analysis is thought to have originated with Sigmund Freud—that is not true, it originated with this emperor one thousand years ago!

In the middle of the night all the prophets of his capital, all the wise men, all those who were concerned in some way with the future—dream readers—were called together and told the story. The story was simple, but they had brought their scriptures and they started arguing with each other: "This cannot be the meaning" or "This is bound to be the meaning."

They wasted time, the sun started rising. The king had an old servant whom he treated as a father, because his father had died very early. The son was too young, and his father had given the guardianship to this servant and told him, "Take care that he becomes my successor and does not lose the kingdom." The servant had managed, and now he was very old. But he was not treated as a servant, he was almost as respected as a father. He came close to the emperor and said, "I want to say two things to you. You have always listened to me. I am not a prophet and I am not an astrologer and I don't know what all this nonsense is that's going on, scriptures being consulted. One thing is certain—that once the sun has risen, the sunset is not very far away. And these people, the so-called knowledgeable people, have never come to any conclusion in centuries. Just in one day . . . they will quarrel, argue, destroy each other's arguments, but you cannot hope that they will come to a consensus, a conclusion.

"Let them have their discussions. My suggestion is, you have the best horse in the world"—those were the days of horses—"you take the horse and escape from this palace as fast as possible. This much is certain, that you should not be here; you should be far away."

It was logical, rational, although very simple. The emperor left the great intelligent and wise people arguing—they did not even notice that he had left. And he certainly had a horse worth an empire. He was very proud of the horse, there was no other horse known of that strength. And there was such a love between the horse and the emperor, such a deep affinity, a kind of synchronicity. The emperor said to the horse, "It seems my death is coming. That shadow was nothing but death. You have to take me as far away from this palace as you can manage."

The horse nodded his head. And he fulfilled his promise. By the evening, as the sun was setting, they were hundreds of miles away from their kingdom. They had entered into another kingdom in disguise. The emperor was very happy. He got down and was tying the horse to a tree—because neither had he eaten anything nor the horse. So he said to the horse, "Thank you, my friend. Now I will make arrangements for your food, for my food. We are so far away, there is no fear. But you proved the stories that were told about you. You moved almost like a cloud, with such speed."

And as he was tying the horse to the tree, the dark shadow appeared and said to the emperor, "I was afraid that you might not be able to make it, but your horse is great. I also thank him—this is the place and this is the time. And I was worried—you were so far away, how could I manage to bring you? The horse served destiny."

It is a strange story, but it shows that wherever you are going horizontally, with whatever speed, you will end up in some graveyard. It is strange that every moment our graves are coming closer to us—even if you don't move, your grave is moving toward you. The horizontal line of time is, in other words, the mortality of man.

But if you can reach to the center of your being, the silences of your innermost center, you can see two roads: one horizontal, another vertical.

You will be surprised to know that the Christian cross is not Christian at all. It is an ancient, Eastern, Aryan symbol—the swastika. That's why Adolf Hitler, who was thinking that he was of the purest Aryan blood, chose the swastika as his symbol. A swastika is nothing but two lines crossing. In India, without knowing why, at the beginning of every year businesspeople will begin their new books with a swastika. The Christian cross is simply a part of the swastika. But it also represents the same thing: the vertical, the horizontal. Christ's hands are horizontal; his head and his being are pointing in a different direction.

In a moment of meditation you suddenly see that you can move in two directions—either horizontal or vertical. The vertical consists of silences, blissfulness, ecstasies; the horizontal consists of hands, work, the world.

Once a man has known himself as a crossroads he cannot be uninterested, he cannot be unintrigued about the vertical. The horizontal he knows, but the vertical opens a door to eternity where death does not exist, where one simply becomes more and more part of the cosmic whole—where one loses all bondages, even the bondage of the body.

Gautam Buddha used to say, "Birth is pain, life is pain, death is pain." What he was saying was that to move on the horizontal line is to be constantly miserable, in pain. Your life cannot be a life of dance, of joy—if this is all, then suicide is the only solution. That's the conclusion the contemporary, Western philosophy of existentialism has come to—the philosophy of Jean Paul Sartre, Jaspers, Heidegger, Kierkegaard, and others—that life is meaningless. And on the horizontal plane it is, because it is simply agony and pain and disease and sickness and oldness. And you are encaged in a small body while your consciousness is as vast as the whole universe.

Once the vertical is discovered, one starts moving on the vertical line. That vertical line does not mean you have to renounce the world, but it certainly means that you are no more of the world, that the world becomes ephemeral, loses importance. It does not mean that you have to renounce the world and escape to the mountains and the monasteries. It simply means that you start—wherever you are—living an inner life that was not possible before.

> In a moment of meditation you suddenly see that you can move in two directions—either horizontal or vertical. The vertical consists of silences, blissfulness, ecstasies; the horizontal consists of hands, work, the world.

e you were an extrovert; now you become an introvert.

ie body is concerned you can manage very easily, if the remembrance is there that you are not the body. But the body can be used in many ways to help you to move on the vertical line.

The penetration of the vertical line, just a ray of light coming into your darkness of horizontal life, is the beginning of enlightenment.

You will look the same but you will not be the same. Those who have a clarity of seeing, to them you will not look the same either—and at least for yourself, you will never look the same and you can never be the same. You will be in the world but the world will not be in you. Ambitions, desires, jealousies will start evaporating. No effort will be needed to drop them, just your movement on the vertical line and they start disappearing—because they cannot exist on the vertical line. They can exist only in the darkness of the horizontal where everybody is in competition, everybody is full of lust, full of will to power, a great desire to dominate, to become somebody special.

On the vertical line all these stupidities simply disappear. You become so light, so weightless, just like a lotus flower—it is in the

> Once the vertical is discovered, one starts moving on the vertical line. That vertical line does not mean you have to renounce the world, but it certainly means that you are no more of the world, that the world becomes ephemeral, loses importance.

water, but the water does not touch it. You remain in the world but the world no longer has any impact on you. On the contrary, you start influencing the world—not with conscious effort but just by your sheer being, your presence, your grace, your beauty. As it grows inside it starts spreading around you.

It will touch people who have an open heart, and it will make people afraid who have lived with a closed heart—all windows, all doors closed. They will not come in contact with such a person. And to convince themselves why they are not coming in contact with such a person, they will find a thousand and one excuses, a thousand and one lies. But the basic fact is that they are afraid to be exposed.

The man who is moving vertically becomes almost a mirror. If you come close to him you will see your real face—you will see your ugliness, you will see your continuous ambitiousness, you will see your begging bowl.

Perhaps another story will help you.

A man, early in the morning, a beggar with a begging bowl, entered the king's garden. The king used to come for a morning walk; otherwise it was impossible to meet the king—particularly for a beggar, the whole bureaucracy would prevent him. So he had chosen a time when there was no bureaucracy and when the king wanted to be alone, in silence with nature, to drink as much beauty and aliveness as nature was showering. The beggar encountered him there.

The king said, "This is not the time . . . I don't see anybody."

The beggar said, "I am a beggar. Your bureaucracy is too difficult and for a beggar it is impossible to see you. I insist that you give me an audience."

The king just thought to get rid of him. He said, "What do you want? Just say and you will get it. Don't disturb my morning silence."

The beggar said, "Think twice before you offer to give me something."

The king said, "You seem to be a strange man. In the first place, you entered without permission into the garden, insisting that you have to have an audience with the king. And now I am saying that whatever you want, just say it. Don't disturb my peace and don't disturb my silence."

The beggar laughed. He said, "A peace that is disturbed is not peace. And a silence that is disturbed is just a dream, not a reality."

Now the king looked at the beggar. He was saying something of tremendous importance. The king thought, "He does not seem to be an ordinary beggar, that is certain." And the beggar said again, "I want you to think it over, because what I want is just for you to fill my begging bowl with anything and I will go. But it has to be full."

The king laughed. He said, "You are a madman. Do you think your begging bowl cannot be filled?" He called his treasurer and told him, "Fill his begging bowl with diamonds, precious stones."

The treasurer had no idea what had happened. Nobody fills beggars' bowls with diamonds. And the beggar reminded the treasurer, "Remember, unless the begging bowl is full I am not going to move from here." It was a challenge between a beggar and a king.

And then there follows a very strange story. . . . As diamonds were poured into the begging bowl, the moment they were poured in they would disappear. The king was in a very embarrassed state.

But he said, "Whatever happens, even if my whole treasury is gone, I cannot be defeated by a beggar. I have defeated great emperors." And the whole treasury disappeared! The rumor reached the capital and thousands of people gathered to see what was happening. They had never seen the king in such a trembling, nervous breakdown.

Finally, when nothing was left in the treasury and the begging bowl was still as empty as it was before, the king fell to the feet of the beggar and said, "You will have to forgive me, I did not understand. I have never thought about these things. I did my best, but now . . . I don't have anything else to offer you. I will think that you have forgiven me if you can tell me the secret of your begging bowl. It is a strange begging bowl—just a few diamonds would have filled it, but it has taken the whole treasury."

The beggar laughed and he said, "You need not be worried. This is not a begging bowl. I found a human skull and out of the human skull I made this begging bowl. It has not forgotten its old habit. Have you looked into your own begging bowl, your own head? Give it anything and it will ask for more and more and more. It knows only one language, 'more.' It is always empty, it is always a beggar."

On the horizontal line only beggars exist, because they are all rushing for more and the more cannot be fulfilled—not that you cannot get to a position you want, but the moment you get it there are higher positions. For a moment maybe a flicker of happiness, and the next moment again the same despair and the same race for more. You cannot fulfill the idea of more. It is intrinsically unfulfillable. And this is the horizontal line, the line of more and more and more.

What is the vertical line? Of being less and less and less, to the point of utter emptiness, to the point of being nobody. Just a signature—not even on sand, but on water; you have not even made it and it has disappeared. The man of the vertical line is the authentic sannyasin, who is immensely happy in being nobody, immensely happy with his inner purity of emptiness because only emptiness can be pure—who is absolutely contented with his nakedness, because only nothingness can be in tune with the universe.

Once this tuning with the universe happens you are no more, in a sense—in the old sense, you are no more. But you are for the first time the whole universe. Even the faraway stars are within you, your nothingness can contain them. The flowers and the sun and the moon . . . and the whole music of existence. You are no more an ego, your "I" has disappeared. But that does not mean that *you* have disappeared. On the contrary, the moment your "I" has disappeared, *you* have appeared.

> You cannot fulfill the idea of more. It is intrinsically unfulfillable. And this is the horizontal line, the line of more and more and more.

It is such a great ecstasy to be without the feeling of "I," without the feeling of any ego, without asking for anything more. What more can you ask? You have nothingness—in this nothingness you have become, without conquering, the whole universe. Then the singing birds are not only singing outside you. They appear outside because this body creates the barrier.

On the vertical line you become more and more consciousness and less and less body. The whole identification with the body disappears. In nothingness, these birds will be within you; these flowers, these trees, and this beautiful morning will be within you. In fact, then there is no "without." Everything has become your vision. And you cannot have a richer life than when everything has become your within. When the sun and the moon and the stars and the whole infinity of time and space is within you . . . what more do you want?

This is exactly the meaning of enlightenment: to become so non-existent as an ego that the whole oceanic existence becomes part of you.

Kabir, a great Indian mystic, was uneducated but has written such tremendously significant statements. One of his statements he corrected before he died. He had written when he was young a beautiful statement. It was, "Just as a dewdrop slips from the lotus leaf in the early morning sun, shining like a pearl, into the ocean . . ." He said, "The same has happened to me." His words are, "I have been searching, my friend. Rather than finding myself, I got lost in the cosmos. The dewdrop disappeared into the ocean." Just before dying, as he was closing his eyes, he asked his son, Kamal, "Please change my statement."

> It is such a great ecstasy to be without the feeling of "I," without the feeling of any ego, without asking for anything more. What more can you ask? You have nothingness—in this nothingness you have become, without conquering, the whole universe.

Kamal said, "I had always suspected that there was something wrong in it." And he showed him his own writing, in which he had already corrected it. The correction—even before Kabir realized—had been done already. That's why Kabir called him Kamal—"You are a miracle." *Kamal* means "miracle." And the man *was* a miracle. He had changed the line that Kabir wanted: "My friend, I was seeking and searching myself. Rather than finding myself I have found the whole world, the whole universe. The dewdrop has not disappeared into the ocean but the ocean has disappeared into the dewdrop."

And when the ocean disappears into the dewdrop, the dewdrop is simply losing its boundaries, nothing else.

On the vertical line, you become less and less and less and less. And one day, you are no more.

A Zen Master, Rinzai, had a very absurd habit, but beautiful. Every morning, when he would wake up, before opening his eyes he would say, "Rinzai, are you still here?"

His disciples said, "What kind of nonsense is this?"

He said, "I am waiting for the moment when the answer will be, 'No. Existence is, but Rinzai is not.' " This is the ultimate peak human consciousness can reach. This is the ultimate benediction. And unless one reaches to this peak, one will remain wandering in dark pathways, blind, suffering, miserable. He may accumulate much knowledge, he may become a great scholar, but that does not help. Only one thing, a very simple thing, is the essence of the whole religious experience, and that is meditation.

You go inward. It will be difficult to get out from the crowd of your thoughts, but you are not a thought. You can get out of the crowd, you can create a distance between you and your thoughts. And as the distance grows bigger, the thoughts start falling like leaves that have died—because it is you and your identity with the thoughts that give them nourishment. When you are not giving them nourishment, thoughts cannot exist. Have you met any thought somewhere standing by itself?

And just try to be indifferent—the word of Gautam Buddha is *upeksha*. Just be indifferent to the whole mind and a distance will be created—and then come to a point from where all nourishment to the thoughts is stopped. They simply disappear; they are soap bubbles. And the moment all thoughts disappear, you will find yourself in the same situation, asking, "Rinzai are you still here?" And you will wait for that great moment, that great, rare opportunity when the answer will be, "No. Who is this guy Rinzai?"

This silence is meditation—and it is not a talent. Everybody cannot be a Picasso, cannot be a Rabindranath, a Michelangelo—those are talents. But everybody can be enlightened because it is not a talent; it is your intrinsic nature, of which you are unaware. And you will remain unaware if you remain surrounded by thoughts. The awareness of your ultimate reality arises only when there is nothing to prevent it, when there is nothingness surrounding you.

The vertical line is rare. It is perhaps the only rare thing in existence, because it takes you on the journey of eternity and immortality. The flowers that blossom on those paths are inconceivable by the mind, and the experiences that happen are unexplainable. But in a very strange way the man himself becomes the expression. His eyes show the depths of his heart, his gestures show the grace of the vertical movement. His whole life radiates, pulsates, and creates a field of energy.

Those who are prejudiced, those who are already determined and concluded . . . I feel sorry for them. But those who are open, unprejudiced, have not concluded yet, they will immediately start feeling the pulsation, the radiation. And a certain synchronicity can happen between the heart of the man of the vertical and the heart of one who is not yet vertical. . . . The moment the synchronicity happens, in that same moment you also start moving vertically.

These are words simply to explain things that are not explainable through words.

> ⤳
>
> Everybody cannot be a Picasso, cannot be a Rabindranath, a Michelangelo—those are talents. But everybody can be enlightened because it is not a talent, it is your intrinsic nature, of which you are unaware.

THE LAWS OF AGING

Everybody is getting old. Since the day you were born you have been getting old—each moment, each day. Childhood is a flux, so is youth—just old age never ends, because it terminates! That is the unique quality of old age, that it brings you to ultimate rest. But if you want a few laws for middle age . . . As far as I am concerned, I have never been a child, never a youth, and never become old and never will die. I know only one thing in me that is absolutely unchanging and eternal. But just for your sake . . .

There are many laws about old age, because all over the world people become old. And many thinkers have been pondering, what is this old age?

The first law is de Never's Last Law; it is obviously about old age, the law can be the first and the last: "Never speculate on that which can be known for certain."

You know perfectly well you are getting old, now don't speculate on it, that will make you more miserable.

The law is beautiful: "Never speculate on that which can be known for certain." In fact, except death nothing is certain in life; everything can be speculated upon, but not death. And old age is just the door to death.

"Middle age is when you begin to exchange your emotions for symptoms."

"You know you are getting old when a girl says no, and all you feel is relief."

"Old age is when you start to turn out the lights for economic rather than romantic reasons."

"Old age is that period of life when your idea of getting ahead is staying even."

"Old age is when you can do just as much as ever, but would rather not."

Old age is a mysterious experience, but all these laws have been found by the western mind. I have not been able to discover anybody in the whole literature of the East talking about old age in this way. On the contrary, old age has been praised immensely. If your life has simply moved on the horizontal line, you are only aged, but if your life, your consciousness, has moved vertically, upward, then you have attained the beauty and the glory of old age. Old age in the East has been synonymous with wisdom.

These are the two paths: one is horizontal, from childhood to youth to old age and to death; another is vertical, from childhood to youth to old age, and to immortality. The difference in quality of both the dimensions is immense, incalculable. The man who simply becomes young and then old and then dead has remained identified with his body. He has not known anything about his being, because being is never born and never dies; it is always, it has been always, it will be always. It is the whole of eternity.

On the vertical line the child becomes a youth, but the youth on the vertical line will be different from the youth on the horizontal line. Childhood is innocent, but that is the point from where these two different dimensions open up. The youth on the horizontal line is nothing but sensuality, sexuality, and all kinds of stupidities. The youth on the vertical line is a search for truth, is a search for life—it is a longing to know oneself.

On the horizontal line, old age is simply trembling, afraid of death; it cannot think of anything except a graveyard and darkness that goes on becoming darker and darker. It cannot conceive of itself except as a skeleton. On the vertical line, old age is a celebration; it is as beautiful as man has ever been.

Youth is a little foolish—is bound to be, it is inexperienced. But old age has passed through all the experiences—good and bad, right and wrong—and has come to a state where it is no longer affected by anything concerned with body or mind. It is a welcome! Old age on the vertical line is keeping its door open for the ultimate guest to come in. It is not an end, it is the beginning of a real life, of an authentic being.

Hence, I continually make the distinction between growing old and growing up. Very few people have been fortunate to grow up. The remainder of humanity has only been growing old—and naturally they are all moving toward death. Only on the vertical line does death not exist; that is the way to immortality, to divinity. And naturally, when one becomes old in that dimension he has a grace and a beauty, a compassion and love.

It has been noted again and again . . . There is a statement in Buddhist scriptures that as Buddha became older he became more beautiful. This I call a true miracle—not walking on water, any drunkard can try that. Not turning water into wine, any criminal can do that. This is a true miracle: Buddha became more beautiful than he was in his youth; he became more innocent than he was in his childhood—this is growth.

Unless you are moving on the vertical line, you are missing the whole opportunity of life. When you move on the vertical line every day you are coming closer to life, not farther away. Then your birth is not the beginning of death, your birth is the beginning of eternal life. Just two different lines and so much difference . . .

The West has never thought about it; the vertical line has never

> On the horizontal line, old age is simply trembling, afraid of death; it cannot think of anything except a graveyard, and darkness which goes on becoming darker and darker. It cannot conceive of itself except as a skeleton. On the vertical line, old age is a celebration; it is as beautiful as man has ever been.

been mentioned because they haven't been brought up in a spiritual atmosphere where the real riches are inside you. Even if they think of God, they think of him outside. Gautam Buddha could deny God—I deny God—there is absolutely no God for the simple reason that we want you to turn inward. If God exists, or anything similar, it has to be found inside you. It has to be found in your own eternity, in your own ecstasy.

To think of oneself as just a body-mind structure is the most dangerous idea that has happened to people. That destroys their whole grace, their whole beauty, and they are constantly trembling and afraid of death and trying to keep old age as far away as possible. In the West, if you say to an old woman, "You look so young," and she knows she is no longer young, she will stand in front of the mirror for hours to check whether any youthfulness has remained anywhere. But she will not deny it, she will be immensely happy. In the East nobody says to an old woman, "You look so young." On the contrary, old age is so respected and loved that to say to somebody, "You look younger than your age," is a kind of insult.

I am reminded of one incident that happened. I was staying with a family, and they were very much interested in a palm reader. They loved me and I used to go at least three times per year to their home and stay there for at least three or four days each time. Once when I went there, without asking they had arranged with the palm reader to come and look at my hands and say some things about me. When I came to know about it, everything was already fixed; the palm reader was sitting in the sitting room. So I said, "Okay, let us enjoy that too!"

I showed him my hand; he pondered over it, and he said, "You must be at least eighty years old." Of course one of the daughters freaked out, "This is stupid. What kind of palm reading . . . ?"

At that time I was not more than thirty-five—even a blind man could have measured the difference between thirty-five and eighty. She was really angry, and she told me, "I am finished with this guy. What else can he know?"

I said, "You don't understand. You are more westernized, educated in the western style. You have been to the West for your education and you can't understand what he was saying."

She said, "What was he saying? It was so clear there is no need to understand; he was simply showing his stupidity. A young man of thirty-five, and he is saying that you are eighty years old?"

I told her a story about Ralph Waldo Emerson. A man asked Emerson, "How old are you?"

Emerson said, "Nearabout three hundred and sixty years." The man could not believe it . . . and he had always believed that Emerson was a man of truth! What had happened, a slip of the tongue? Had he become senile? Or was he joking?

To make things clear he said, "I did not hear what you said. Just tell me how much . . . ?"

> In the East nobody says to an old woman, "You look so young"—on the contrary, old age is so respected and loved that to say to somebody "You look younger than your age" is a kind of insult.

Emerson said, "You have heard it—three hundred and sixty years."

The man said, "I cannot believe it. You don't look more than sixty years."

Emerson said, "You are right in a way: on the vertical I am three hundred and sixty, and on the horizontal I am sixty."

Perhaps he was the first western man to use this expression of horizontal and vertical. Emerson was immensely interested in the East, and he had a few glimpses that brought him closer to the seers of the Upanishads. He said, "Actually I have lived sixty years; you are right. But in sixty years I have lived as much as you will not be able to live even in three hundred and sixty years. I have lived six times more."

The vertical line does not count years, it counts your experiences. And on the vertical line is the whole treasure of existence—not only immortality, not only a feeling of godliness, but the first experience of love without hate, the first experience of compassion, the first experience of meditation—the first experience of the tremendous explosion of enlightenment.

It is not a coincidence that in the West, the word *enlightenment* does not have the same meaning as in the East. They say that after the dark ages came the age of enlightenment. They refer to people like Bertrand Russell, Jean Paul Sartre, Karl Jaspers as enlightened geniuses. They don't understand that they are misusing a word, dragging it into the mud. Neither is Bertrand Russell enlightened nor Jean Paul Sartre nor Karl Jaspers.

Enlightenment does not happen on the horizontal line. Even in his old age Jean Paul Sartre was still running after young girls.

Bertrand Russell changed his wife so many times—and he lived long on the horizontal line, almost a century. But even in his old age, his interests were as stupid as young people's.

The East understands that the word *enlightenment* has nothing to do with genius, has nothing to do with intellect, it has something to do with discovering your real, authentic being. It is discovering God within you.

So you need not be worried about laws. Those laws are all on the horizontal line. On the vertical line there is love, no law. There is the growing experience of becoming more and more spiritual and less and less physical, more and more meditative and less and less mind, more and more divine and less and less of this trivial material world in which we are so much enmeshed.

On the vertical line, slowly you feel desires disappearing, sexuality disappearing, ambitions disappearing, will to power disappearing . . . your slavery in all its aspects disappearing—religious, political, national. You become more of an individual. And with your individuality growing clear and luminous, the whole humanity is becoming one in your eyes—you cannot discriminate.

There are great experiences on the vertical line; on the hori-

> The word *enlightenment* has nothing to do with genius, has nothing to do with intellect. It has something to do with discovering your real, authentic being. It is discovering God within you.

zontal line there is only decline. On the horizontal line the old man lives in the past. He thinks of those beautiful days, those Arabian nights when he was young. He thinks also of those beautiful days when there was no responsibility and he was a child running after butterflies. In fact, for his whole life he has been running after butterflies—even in old age.

On the horizontal line, that's what happens—as you grow old you become more and more infatuated by desires, because now you know that ahead there is only death. So you want to enjoy as much as possible, although enjoying becomes difficult because physically you have lost the energy. So the old man on the horizontal line becomes cerebrally sexual; he is continuously thinking of sex. The old man has nothing else to do but to think—and what else is there to think about? He imagines beautiful women.

The old man is continuously thinking of the past—this is the psychology. The child thinks of the future because he has no past; there is no question of thinking of the past—he has no yesterday. He thinks of days to come, the whole long life. Seventy years gives him space. . . . He wants to become big enough quickly to do things that all the big people are doing.

The old man has no future—the future means death, he does not even want to talk about the future. The future makes him tremble, the future means the grave—he talks about the past.

And the same is true about countries. For example, a country like India never thinks of the future. That means it has become old; it is symptomatic. India always thinks of the past. It goes on playing dramas of the life of Rama and Sita, for centuries the same story . . . every village performs that drama. It goes on thinking about Buddha and Mahavira and Adinatha, and the Rigveda and the Upanishads. Everything has passed. Now the country is simply waiting to die; there is no future.

According to the Indian idea—and that is the idea of the old mentality, the mind of the old man— the best age was millions of years ago; it was called *satyuga*, the age of truth. After that man started falling. You can see the psychological parallel; there are four ages: childhood, the young man, middle age, the old man. According to these four he has projected four ages for life itself. The first age was innocent, just like a child, very balanced. They give the example that it has four legs just like a table, perfectly balanced. And then the decline starts. . . .

In India, the idea of evolution has never existed, but on the contrary just the opposite idea. The word is not even used in the West—you may not have even heard of the word— but in India they have been thinking

> The child thinks of the future, of the golden future, the old man thinks of the golden past. But this happens only on the horizontal line. On the vertical line, the past is golden, the present is golden, the future is golden, it is a life of tremendous celebration.

about devolution, not evolution: "We are shrinking, we are falling down." In the second stage of the fall, one leg is lost; the table becomes a tripod. It is still balanced, but not as much as it was with four legs. In the third stage it loses another leg; now it is standing only on two legs, absolutely unbalanced. And this is the fourth stage: even two legs are not available; you are standing on one leg—how long you can stand?

The first stage is called *satyuga*, the age of truth. The second is simply named by the number; *treta* is the third, because only three legs are left. The third stage is called *dwapar*. *Dwa* is a Sanskrit word—moving through many other languages it finally it becomes "two." And the fourth age they have called *kaliyuga*, the age of darkness.

We are living in the age of darkness—this is the mind of the old man, that ahead there is only darkness and nothing else. The child thinks of the future, of the golden future; the old man thinks of the golden past. But this happens only on the horizontal line. On the vertical line, the past is golden, the present is golden, the future is golden; it is a life of tremendous celebration.

So rather than being worried about the laws of old age, think about which line your train is moving on. There is still time to change trains; there is always time to change trains because from every moment that bifurcation is available. You can shift, shift from the horizontal to the vertical; only that is important.

SYMPTOMS

~

THE STRANGER IN THE DRAWING ROOM

An older woman says she has noticed a change in her behavior that she finds disturbing. "I'm aware of great anger sometimes, for not much reason. It passes over very quickly, but I was not aware of it before. Perhaps I always had it . . . ?

No, but it happens after a certain age that polarities change. It is a very subtle process.

Every man has a woman in the unconscious, and every woman has a man in the unconscious. Consciously you are a woman so you use your female faculties—and the more you use them the more exhausted they are. But the unused unconscious remains very young and fresh. When the female part has been used too much, by and by it becomes weaker and then a moment comes when it is so weak that the unconscious male part becomes stronger than the female.

In the beginning the female was the stronger part—that's why you were a woman. For example, you were seventy percent woman, thirty percent man—the thirty percent was repressed, forced into the unconscious by the seventy percent woman. Continuous use of the woman makes this conscious part weaker and weaker and weaker. A moment comes when it falls below thirty percent—then suddenly the wheel turns and the stronger part takes over. It becomes very strong, and you are surprised because you never knew about it before. And the same happens to men—men become feminine as they grow older.

Somewhere nearabout the age of forty-nine, at the age of menopause, the balance in woman starts changing. Once the monthly periods stop, the balance starts changing. Sooner or later one finds a very new being coming in... strange. One is puzzled, confused, because one does not know how to live with this stranger. This stranger has always been there—but it has always been in the basement. It was never part of your household affairs; it has never come upstairs. Now suddenly it comes out of the basement— not only that, it sits in the drawing room and tries to possess everything! And it is powerful.

So the only thing is to accept it, watch it. Don't fight with it, don't try to repress it. You cannot repress it now. Just become more and more aware of it, and this awareness will bring a totally new attitude. You will know that you are neither man nor woman. It was also just a role to be a woman—now it is superseded by another role; the rejected part has surfaced. The conquered part has become the conqueror now. But you are neither— that's why this game is possible.

> Everything that comes has to go. Everything that arises has to fall. Every wave that arises has to disappear, there must be a time when it goes. At fourteen sex comes, at forty-nine or thereabouts it goes.

If you were really completely a woman, the male energies could not take possession of you. You were neither woman nor man— one day it was the female part that was more powerful; it played the role. Now the other part is trying to play the role. All old women become more masculine—that's why mothers-in-law are so dangerous! It is a natural thing that happens; nothing can be done about it. You have only to be aware.

You have to watch and stand aloof and see the whole game. Then a third entity, which is neither, becomes clear—you are just a witnessing self, a witnessing soul.

Maleness is in the body, femaleness is in the body—the mind follows shadows, reflections. Deeper in your core, in the very core of your being, you are neither—neither man nor woman. Now that fact has to be understood—once it is understood you can laugh at the whole thing. And once it is understood the whole power of anger, of hardness, will dis-

> Old women become more masculine—that's why mothers-in-law are so dangerous! It is a natural thing that happens, nothing can be done about it. You only have to be aware.

appear. You will not become a woman again but you will not be a man either. You will become totally different.

And this is what one really is. This is what religions call transcendence, surpassing—and man is the only animal who is capable of surpassing himself. That's his beauty—that he can surpass man, woman, this role, that role, good, bad, moral, immoral. He can surpass all and come to a point where he is only pure consciousness, just a watcher on the hill. So don't be worried about it—just watch it. Just be happy!

MENOPAUSE—IT'S NOT JUST A "GIRL THING"

A forty-eight-year-old man says he has a sexual block, which he experiences as an unwillingness to say what he really wants when he is with a woman. He has noticed too, that his sexuality seems to be on the decline.

> Deeper in your core, in the very core of your being you are neither—neither man nor woman. Now that fact has to be understood—once it is understood you can laugh at the whole thing. And once it is understood the whole power of anger, of hardness, will disappear.

This is the time, mm? Somewhere around forty-nine years there comes a menopause for men too, not only for women. The man's menopause is very subtle but it is there—now even scientific research says so. This has been a known fact for Tantra for centuries . . . because basically the man's chemistry and the woman's chemistry cannot be that different. It is different, but it cannot be *that* different.

When a woman becomes sexually mature around twelve, thirteen, fourteen, a man becomes mature around the same time. Then it will be very unfair that the woman has a menopause around forty-nine and that man has no menopause; that will simply prove that God is also a male chauvinist! That is unfair and that is not possible.

There is a difference with men—that's why it has never been detected up to now—but within these past few years much research has been done and they have come to feel that there is a male menopause. And just as the woman has the monthly periods after each twenty-eight days, a man has periods too. For three or four days the woman goes into a depressive state, into a negative state—so does a man. But because the woman's blood is visible there is no need to wonder so much about it—and the woman knows that her period has come, and that the depression and the negativity and everything arise and she becomes very dark, dismal inside.

Man's release is not that visible, but a certain energy is released each month—for three or four days a man also becomes a victim of depression, negativity. If you keep a record for a few months you will be able to see that exactly after twenty-eight days

> It will be very unfair that the woman has a menopause around forty-nine and that man has no menopause, that will simply prove that God is also a male chauvinist! That is unfair and that is not possible.

you again become negative for three or four days—out of the blue, for no reason at all. Just keep a small diary and it will become clear to you. And it happens around forty-nine that menopause comes closer—nothing to be worried about, it is natural. Sexual energies decline—but with the decline of sexual energies, spiritual energies can increase. If one takes a right step, then the declining energy of sexuality can become rising energies of spirituality—because it is the same energy that can move upward. And when sexual interest lessens, there is a greater possibility of uplifting your energies.

So don't take it in a negative way—it can prove a great blessing; just accept it. And there is no need to work upon it, just accept it. Let it be so and don't think in terms of "blocks"—that will be wrong. If a young man of twenty or twenty-five feels a decline in sexual energy,

> *The declining energy of sexuality can become rising energies of spirituality—because it is the same energy that can move upward.*

then there is a block, then something has to be done. If a man after forty-nine does not feel a sexual decline, then something is wrong. Something has to be done—that means he is not moving upward, he is stuck.

And in the West it has become a problem, because in the West sex seems to be the only life. So the moment sexual energy starts declining a man almost feels he is dying. In the East we feel very happy when the sexual energy declines, tremendously happy, because one is finished with that turmoil and that nightmare.

Nothing to be worried about—there is no block there. Within one year things will settle and you will come onto a higher plane: you will be able to see life in a different light and in a different color. Men will not be so much like men and women will not be so much like women. There will be more human beings in the world rather than men and women . . . and that is a totally different world—of human beings. In fact, to look at a woman as woman, at a man as man is not right—but sex creates that division. When sex is no longer a dividing force, you see human beings.

THE DIRTY OLD MAN

It is because of a long, long history of repressiveness in society that the dirty old man exists. It is because of your saints, your priests, your puritans that the old dirty man exists.

If people are allowed to live their sexual life joyously, by the time they are nearing forty-two—remember, I am saying forty-two, not eighty-four—just when they are nearing forty-two, sex will start losing its grip on them. Just as sex arises and becomes very powerful by the time one is fourteen, in exactly the same way by the time one is forty-two it starts disappearing. It is a natural course. And when sex disappears, the old man has a love, has a compassion, of a totally different kind. There is no lust in his love, no desire; he wants to get nothing out of it. His love has a purity, an innocence; his love is a joy.

> In fact to look at a woman as woman, at a man as man, is not right—but sex creates that division. When sex is no longer a dividing force, you see human beings.

Sex gives you pleasure. And sex gives you pleasure only when you have gone into sex; then pleasure is the end result. If sex has become irrelevant—not repressed, but because you experienced it so deeply that it is no more of any value . . . you have known it, and knowledge always brings freedom. You have known it totally, and because you have known it, the mystery is finished, there is nothing more to explore. In that knowing, the whole energy, the sexual energy, is transmuted into love, compassion. One gives out of joy. Then the old man is the most beautiful man in the world, the cleanest man in the world.

> If people are allowed to live their sexual life joyously, by the time they are nearing forty-two—remember, I am saying forty-two, not eighty-four—just when they are nearing forty-two, sex will start losing its grip on them.

There is no expression in any language like the "clean old man." I have never heard it. But this expression, the "dirty old man," exists in almost all languages. The reason is that the body becomes old, the body becomes tired, the body wants to get rid of all sexuality—but the mind, because of repressed desires, still hankers. When the body is not capable and the mind continuously haunts you for something that the body is incapable of doing, really the old man is in a mess. His eyes are sexual, lusty; his body dead and dull. And his mind goes on goading him. He starts having a dirty look, a dirty face; he starts having something ugly in him.

It reminds me of the story of the man who overheard his wife and her sister discussing his frequent out-of-town business trips. The sister kept suggesting that the wife should worry about her husband being unchaperoned at those posh resort convention hotels with so many attractive, unattached career women around.

"Me worry?" said the wife. "Why, he'd never cheat on me. He's too loyal, too decent . . . too old."

The body sooner or later becomes old; it is bound to become old. But if you have not lived your desires they will clamor around you, they are bound to create something ugly in you. Either the old man becomes the most beautiful man in the world, because he attains to an innocence the same as the innocence of a child, or even far deeper than the innocence of a child . . . he becomes a sage. But if desires are still there, running like an undercurrent, then he is caught in a turmoil.

A very old man was arrested while attempting to sexually molest a young woman. Seeing such an old man, eighty-four, in court, the magistrate reduced the charge from rape to assault with a dead weapon.

If you are becoming old, remember that old age is the climax of life. Remember that old age can be the most beautiful experience— because the child has hopes for the future, he lives in the future, he has great desires to do this, to do that. Every child thinks that he is going to be somebody special—Alexander the Great, Josef Stalin, Mao Zedong—he lives in desires and in the future. The young man is too much possessed by the instincts, all instincts exploding in him. Sex is there—modern research says that every man thinks about sex at least once every three minutes. Women are a little better, they think of sex every six minutes. It is a great difference, almost double— that may be the cause of many rifts between husbands and wives!

Once every three minutes sex somehow flashes in the mind— the young man is possessed by such great natural forces that he cannot be free. Ambition is there, and time is running fast, and he has to do something and he has to be something. All those hopes and desires and fantasies of childhood have to be fulfilled; he is in a great rush, in a hurry.

The old man knows that those childish desires were really childish. The old man knows that all those days of youth and turmoil are gone. The old man is in the same state as when the storm has gone and silence prevails—that silence can be of tremendous beauty, depth, richness. If the old man is really mature, which is very rarely the case, then he will be beautiful. But people only grow in age, they don't grow up. Hence the problem.

> ❧
>
> This expression, "the dirty old man," exists in almost all languages. The body becomes old, the body becomes tired, wants to get rid of all sexuality—but the mind, because of repressed desires, still hankers.

Grow up, become more mature, become more alert and aware. And old age is the last opportunity given to you: before death comes, prepare. And how does one prepare for death? By becoming more meditative.

If some lurking desires are still there, and the body is getting old and the body is not capable of fulfilling those desires, don't be worried. Meditate over those desires, watch, be aware. Just by being aware and watchful and alert, those desires and the energy contained in them can be transmuted. But before death comes, be free of all desires.

When I say be free of all desires I simply mean be free of all *objects* of desire. Then there is a pure longing—that pure longing is divine, that pure longing is God. Then there is pure creativity with no object, with no address, with no direction, with no destination—just pure energy, a pool of energy going nowhere. That's what buddhahood is.

BITTERNESS

We are bitter because we are not what we should be. Everybody is feeling sour because everybody is feeling this is not what life should be; if this is all, then this is nothing. There must be something more to it, and unless that something more is found one cannot drop one's bitterness. Out of this bitterness comes anger, jealousy, violence, hatred—all kinds of negativities. One is continuously complaining, but the real complaint is somewhere else deep down. It is a complaint against existence: "What am I doing here? Why am I here? Nothing is happening. Why am I forced to be alive, because nothing is happening." Time goes on passing and life remains without any bliss. It creates bitterness.

It is not accidental that old people become very bitter. It is very difficult to live with old people, even if they are your own parents. It is very difficult for the simple reason that their whole life has gone down the drain and they are feeling bitter. They jump upon any excuse to throw their negativity; they start catharting and freaking out over anything. They cannot tolerate children being happy, dancing, singing, shouting with joy—they cannot tolerate it. It is a nuisance for them because they have missed their life. And in fact when they are saying, "Don't be a nuisance to us," they are simply saying, "How dare you be so joyous!" They are against young people, and whatsoever the young people are doing the old always think they are wrong.

In fact, they are simply feeling bitter about the whole thing called life, and they go on finding excuses. It is very rare to find an old person who is not bitter—that means he has lived really beautifully, he is really a grown up. Then old people have tremendous beauty, which no young man can ever have. They have a certain ripeness, maturity, they are seasoned. They have seen so much and lived so much that they are tremendously grateful to God.

But it is very hard to find that type of old man, because it means that man is a Buddha, a Christ. Only an awakened person can be nonbitter in old age—because death is coming, life is gone, what is there for one to be happy about? One is simply angry.

> You have heard about angry young men, but really no young man can ever be as angry as old people. Nobody talks about angry old men but my own experience is that nobody can be as angry as the old.

You have heard about angry young men, but really no young man can ever be as angry as old people. Nobody talks about angry old men, but my own experience—I have watched young people, old people— is that nobody can be as angry as the old.

Bitterness is a state of ignorance. You have to go beyond it, you have to learn the awareness that becomes a bridge to take you beyond. And that very going is a revolution. The moment you have really gone beyond all complaints, all nos, a tremendous yes arises—just yes, yes, yes—there is great fragrance. The same energy that was bitter becomes fragrance.

TRANSITIONS

༄

FROM NO TO YES

Consciousness brings freedom. Freedom does not mean only the freedom to do right; if that were the meaning of freedom, what kind of freedom would it be? If you are free only to do right, then you are not free. Freedom implies both the alternatives—to do right, to do wrong. Freedom implies the right to say yes or to say no.

And this is something subtle to be understood: saying no feels like more of a freedom than saying yes. And I am not philosophizing, it is a simple fact you can observe in yourself. Whenever you say no, you feel more free. Whenever you say yes, you don't feel free because yes means you have obeyed, yes means you have surrendered—where is the freedom? No means you are stubborn, keeping aloof; no means you have asserted yourself, no means you are ready to fight. No defines you more clearly than yes. Yes is vague, it is like a cloud. No is very solid and substantial, like a rock.

That's why psychologists say that between seven and fourteen years of age each child starts learning to say no more and more. By saying no, he is getting out of the psychological womb of the mother. Even when there is no need to say no, he will say no. Even when to say yes is in his favor, he will say no. There is much at stake; he has to learn to say no more and more. By the time he is fourteen, sexually mature, he will say the ultimate no to the mother—he will fall in love with a woman. That is his ultimate no to the mother, he is turning his back on the mother. He says, "I am finished with you, I have chosen a woman. I have become an individual, independent in my own right. I want to live my life, I want to do my own thing."

And if the parents insist, "Have short hair," he will have long hair. If the parents insist, "Have long hair," he will have short hair. Just watch . . . when hippies become parents then they will see, their children will have short hair because they will have to learn no.

If the parents insist "Cleanliness is next to godliness," the children will start living in every kind of dirt. They will be dirty, they won't take a bath; they won't clean themselves, they won't use soap. And they will find rationalizations that soap is dangerous to the skin, that it is unnatural, that no animal ever uses soap. They can find as many rationalizations as possible, but deep down all those rationalizations are just cover-ups. The real thing is, they want to say no. And of course when you want to say no, you have to find reasons.

Hence, no gives you a sense of freedom; not only that, it also gives you a sense of intelligence. To say yes needs no intelligence. When you say yes, nobody asks you why. When you have already said yes, who bothers to ask you why? There is no need of any reasoning or argument, you have already said yes. When you say no, why is bound to be asked. It sharpens your intelligence, it gives you a definition, a style, freedom.

Watch the psychology of the no. It is so hard for human beings to be in harmony, and it is because of consciousness. Consciousness gives freedom, freedom gives you the capacity to say no, and there is more possibility to say no than to say yes.

Without yes, there is no harmony; yes is harmony. But it takes time to grow up, to mature, to come to such a maturity where you can say yes and yet remain free, where you can say yes and yet remain unique, where you can say yes and yet not become a slave.

The freedom that is brought by no is a very childish freedom. It is good for seven-year-olds up to fourteen-year-olds. But if a person gets caught in it and his whole life becomes a no saying, then he has stopped growing.

The ultimate growth is to say yes with such joy as a child says no. That is a second childhood. And the man who can say yes with tremendous freedom and joy, with no hesitation, with no strings attached, with no conditions—a pure and simple joy, a pure and simple yes—that man has become a sage. That man lives in harmony again, and his harmony is of a totally different dimension from the harmony of trees, animals, and birds. They live in harmony because they *cannot* say no, and the sage lives in harmony because he *does not* say no. Between the two, the birds and the buddhas, are all human beings—un-grown up, immature, childish, stuck somewhere, still trying to say no, to have some feeling of freedom.

> It takes time to grow up, to mature, to come to such a maturity where you can say yes and yet remain free, where you can say yes and yet remain unique, where you can say yes and yet not become a slave.

I am not saying don't learn to say no. I am saying learn to say no when it is time to say no but don't get stuck with it. Slowly slowly, see that there is a higher freedom that comes with yes, and a greater harmony.

The ultimate growth is to say yes with such joy as a child says no. That is a second childhood. And the man who can say yes with tremendous freedom and joy, with no hesitation, with no strings attached, with no conditions—a pure and simple joy, a pure and simple yes— that man has become a sage.

INTEGRATION AND CENTERING

Integration is already there at the deepest core of your being. At your very center you are integrated, otherwise you could not exist at all. How can you exist without a center? The cart moves because there is an unmoving center on which the wheel moves—it moves on the hub. If the cart is moving the hub is there. You may know it, you may not know it.

You are alive, you are breathing, you are conscious; life is moving, so there must be a hub to the wheel of life. You may not be aware, but it is there. Without it, you cannot be.

So the first thing and very fundamental: becoming is not the issue. You are. You have just to go in and see it. It is a discovery, not an achievement. You have been carrying it all along. But you have become too attached to the periphery, and your back is to the center. You have become too outgoing, so you cannot look in.

Create a little insight. The word *insight* is beautiful—it means "sight in, to look in, to see in." Eyes open outward, hands spread outward, legs move away from you. Sit silently, relax the periphery, close your eyes and just go in . . . and not with effort. Just relax— as if one is drowning and one cannot do anything. We go on doing even when we are drowning.

If you can simply allow it to happen, it will come to the surface. Out of the clouds you will see the center arising.

There are two modes of life. One is the action mode—you do something. The other is the reception mode—you simply receive. The action mode is outgoing. If you want more money you cannot just sit. It is not going to come that way. You will have to struggle for it, compete, and you will have to use all sorts of ways and means—legal, illegal, right, wrong. Money is not going to come by just sitting. If you want to become powerful, if you want to become a politician, you will have to do something about it. It is not going to come on its own.

> You are. You have just to go in and see it. It is a discovery, not an achievement. You have been carrying it all along.

There is an action mode; the action mode is the outgoing mode. And there is an inaction mode too: you don't do anything, you simply allow it to happen. We have forgotten that language. That forgotten language has to be learned again.

Integration has not to be brought in—it is already there. We have forgotten how to look at it, we have forgotten how to understand it. Move from the action mode more and more to the receptive, passive mode.

I'm not saying to leave the world of action—because that will make you lopsided again. You are lopsided right now. You have only one mode to your life, and that is action, doing something. There are people who cannot think of sitting silently; it is impossible. They cannot allow themselves a moment's relaxation. They are interested only in action. If something is being done, then they are interested. If it is just a sunset, then what is the point of looking at it?

> There is an action mode—the action mode is the outgoing mode. And there is an inaction mode too: you don't do anything, you simply allow it to happen. We have forgotten that language. That forgotten language has to be learned again.

You are interested only in action, if something is happening. This has become too fixed. This has to be relaxed a little: you have to go for a few moments, for a few hours, sometimes for a few days, totally to the other mode of life, just sitting and allowing things to happen. When you look at a sunset you are not expected to do anything. You simply look. When you look at a flower, what are you supposed to do? You simply look.

In fact there is no effort, even of looking at the flower. It is effortless. Your eyes are open, the flower is there . . . a moment of deep communion comes when the looked at and the looker both disappear. Then there is beauty, then there is benediction. Then suddenly you are not the observer, and the flower is not the observed—because to observe there must still be some action. Now you are there and the flower is there, and somehow you overlap each other's boundaries. The flower enters into you, you enter into the flower, and there is a sudden revelation. Call it beauty, call it truth, call it God.

These rare moments have to be allowed more and more. I cannot say they have to be cultivated, I cannot say you have to train for those moments, I cannot say that you have to do something—because again that will be using the language of the action mode and will be very deeply misinterpreted. No, I can simply say to allow these moments more and more. Sometimes, simply don't do anything. Relax on the lawn and look at the sky. Sometimes close the eyes and just look at your inner world—thoughts moving, floating; desires arising, going. Look at the colorful dream world that goes on within you. Just look. Don't say, "I want to stop these thoughts"—again you have moved into the action mode. Don't say, "I am meditating—go! All thoughts, go away from me"— because if you start saying that, you have started doing something. As if you are not . . .

There is one of the most ancient meditations still used in some monasteries of Tibet. The meditation is based on the truth that I am saying to you. They teach that sometimes you can simply disappear. Sitting in the garden, you just start feeling that you are disappearing. Just see how the world looks when you have gone from the world, when you are no longer here, when you have become absolutely transparent. Just try for a single second not to be.

your own home, be as if you are not.

Just think, one day you will not be. One day you will be gone, you will be dead; the radio will still continue, the wife will still prepare the breakfast, the children will still be getting ready for school. Think: today you are gone, you just are not. Become a ghost. Just sitting in your chair, you simply disappear, you simply think, "I have no more reality; I am not." And just see how the house continues. There will be tremendous peace and silence. Everything will continue as it is. Without you, everything will continue as it is. Nothing will be missed. Then what is the point of always remaining occupied, doing something, doing something, obsessed with action? What is the point? You will be gone, and whatsoever you have done will disappear—as if you had signed your name on the sands, and the wind comes, and the signature disappears . . . and everything is finished. Be as if you had never existed.

> Sitting in the garden, just start feeling that you are disappearing. Just see how the world looks when you have gone from the world, when you are no longer here, when you have become absolutely transparent. Just try for a single second not to be.

It is really a beautiful meditation. You can try it many times in twenty-four hours. Just half a second will do; for half a second, simply stop . . . you are not . . . and the world continues. When you become more and more alert to the fact that without you the world continues perfectly well, then you will be able to learn another part of your being that has been neglected for long, for lives—and that is the receptive mode. You simply allow, you become a door. Things go on happening without you.

This is what Buddha means when he says, "Become a driftwood. Float in the stream like timber, and wherever the stream goes let it take you; you don't make any effort." The whole Buddhist approach belongs to the receptive mode. That's why you see Buddha sitting under a tree. All his images are of sitting, sitting and doing nothing. He's simply sitting there, he's not doing anything.

You don't have that type of image of Jesus. He still goes on following the action mode. That's where Christianity has missed the deepest possibility: Christianity became active. The Christian missionary goes on serving the poor, goes to the hospital, does this and that, and his whole effort is to do something good. Yes, very good— but he remains in the action mode, and God can only be known only in the receptive mode. So a Christian missionary will be a good man, a very good man, but not, in the eastern sense, a saint.

It is really a beautiful meditation. You can try it many times in twenty-four hours. Just half a second will do, for half a second, simply stop...you are not... and the world continues. When you become more and more alert to the fact that without you the world continues perfectly well, then you will be able to learn another part of your being.

Now even in the East a person who goes on doing things is worshiped as a Mahatma—because the East is poor, ill. There are thousands of lepers, blind people, uneducated people; they need education, they need medicine, they need service, they need a thousand and one things. Suddenly the active person has become important—so Gandhi is a Mahatma, and Mother Teresa of Calcutta has become very important. But nobody looks at whether they have attained to the receptive mode or not.

Now if Buddha comes, nobody is going to pay respect to him, because he will not be running a school or a hospital. He will again be sitting under a bodhi tree, just sitting silently. Not that nothing is done by him—tremendous vibes are created by his being, but they are very subtle. He transforms the whole world by sitting under his bodhi tree, but to look at those vibrations you will have to be attuned, you will have to grow. To recognize a Buddha is to be already on the path. To recognize a Mother Teresa is very easy, there is nothing much in it. Anybody can see that she is doing good work.

To do good work is one thing, and to be good is totally another. I'm not saying don't do good works. I am saying: let good works come out of your *being* good.

First attain to the receptive mode, first attain to the passive, first attain to the nonactive. And when your inner being flowers and you have come to know the integration inside—which is always there, the center is always there—when you have recognized that center, suddenly death disappears for you. Suddenly all worries disappear because you are no longer a body now and no longer a mind.

Then compassion arises, love arises, prayer arises. You become a showering, a blessing to the world. Now, nobody can say what will happen to such a man—whether he will go and become a revolutionary like Jesus and chase the moneylenders from the temple, or whether he will go and serve poor people, or whether he will just continue sitting under the bodhi tree and spreading his fragrance, or whether he will become a Meera and dance and sing the glory of God. Nobody knows, it is unpredictable.

My whole effort here is to make you aware that nothing is needed, nothing more is needed. You have it already there, existing inside you. But you have to make approaches, doors, ways to discover it. You have to dig for it; the treasure is there.

I would like to give you a technique. It is a very simple technique, but in the beginning it looks very hard. If you try, you will find it is simple. If you don't try and only think about it, it will look very hard. The technique is: do only that which you enjoy. If you don't enjoy, don't do it. Try it—because enjoyment comes only from your center. If you are doing something and you enjoy it, you start getting reconnected with

> To do good work is one thing, and to be good is totally another. I'm not saying don't do good works. I am saying let good works come out of your *being* good.

the center. If you do something you don't enjoy, you are disconnected from the center. Joy arises from the center and from nowhere else. So let it be a criterion, and be a fanatic about it.

You are walking on the road; suddenly you recognize that you are not enjoying the walk. Stop. Finished—this is not to be done.

I used to do it in my university days, and people thought that I was crazy. Suddenly I would stop, and then I would remain in that spot for half an hour, an hour, unless I started enjoying walking again. My professors were so afraid that when there were examinations they would put me in a car and take me to the university hall. They would leave me at the door and wait there: Had I reached to my desk or not? If I was taking my bath and suddenly I realized that I was not enjoying it, I would stop. What is the point then? If I was eating and I recognized suddenly that I was not enjoying, then I would stop.

I had joined the mathematics class in my high school. The first day, I went in and the teacher was just introducing the subject. In the middle I stood up and tried to walk out. He said, "Where are you going? Without asking, I won't allow you in again." I said, "I'm not coming back again; don't be worried. That's why I am not asking. Finished—I am not enjoying it! I will find some other subject that I can enjoy, because if I cannot enjoy it I am not going to do it. It is torture, it is violence."

> Only do that which you enjoy. If you don't enjoy, don't do it. Try it—because enjoyment comes only from your center. If you are doing something and you enjoy it, you start getting reconnected with the center. Joy arises from the center, and from nowhere else. So let it be a criterion, and be a fanatic about it.

And, by and by, it became a key. I suddenly recognized that whenever you are enjoying something, you are centered. Enjoyment is just the sound of being centered. Whenever you are not enjoying something, you are off center. Then don't force it; there is no need. If people think you crazy, let them think you crazy. Within a few days you will, by your own experience, find how you were missing yourself. You were doing a thousand and one things, that you never enjoyed, and still you were doing them because you were taught to. You were just fulfilling your duties.

People have destroyed even such a beautiful thing as love. You come home and you kiss your wife because it has to be so, it has to be done. Now, a beautiful thing like a kiss, a flowerlike thing, has been destroyed. By and by, without enjoying it, you will go on kissing your wife; you will forget the joy of kissing another human being. You shake hands with anybody you meet—cold, with no meaning in it, with no message in it, no warmth flowing. It is just dead hands shaking each other and saying hello. Then you start, by and by, learning this dead gesture, this cold gesture. You become frozen, you become an ice cube. And then you say, "How to enter to the center?"

> Whenever you are enjoying something, you are centered. Enjoyment is just the sound of being centered.

The center is available when you are warm, when you are flowing, melting, in love, in joy, in dance, in delight. It is up to you. Just go on doing only those things that you *really* love to do and you enjoy. If you don't enjoy, stop. Find something else that you will enjoy. There is bound to be something that you will enjoy. I have never come across a person who cannot enjoy anything. There are persons who may not enjoy one thing, then another, then another, but life is vast. Don't remain engaged; become floating. Let there be more streaming of energy. Let it flow, let it meet with other energies that surround you. Soon you will be able to see that the problem was not how to become integrated, the problem was that you have forgotten how to flow. In a flowing energy, you are suddenly integrated. It happens sometimes accidentally too, but the reason is the same.

> Let there be more streaming of energy. Let it flow, let it meet with other energies that surround you. Soon you will be able to see that the problem was not how to become integrated, the problem was that you have forgotten how to flow.

Sometimes you fall in love with a woman or a man, and suddenly you feel integrated, suddenly you feel you are one for the first time. Your eyes have a glow, your face has a radiance, and your intellect is no longer dull. Something starts burning bright in your being; a song arises, your walk has a quality of dance in it now. You are a totally different being.

But these are rare moments— because we don't learn the secret. The secret is that there must be something you have started to enjoy. That's the whole secret. A painter may be hungry and painting, and still you can see that his face is so contented. A poet may be poor, but when he is singing his song he is the richest man in the world. Nobody is richer than he is. What is the secret of it? The secret is that he is enjoying this moment. Whenever you enjoy something, you are in tune with yourself and you are in tune with the universe—because your center is the center of all.

So let this small insight be a climate for you: do only that which you enjoy, otherwise stop. You are reading a newspaper and halfway through it you suddenly recognize that you are not enjoying it, then there is no necessity. Then why are you reading? Stop it here and now. If you are talking to somebody and in the middle you recognize that you are not enjoying it, you have just said half a sentence, stop then and there. You are not enjoying, you are not obliged to continue. In the beginning it will look a little weird. But I don't think there is any problem. You can practice it.

Within a few days many contacts will be made with the center, and then you will understand what I mean when I go on repeating again and again that that which you are seeking is already in you. It is not in the future. It has nothing to do with the future. It is already herenow, it is already the case.

> Whenever you enjoy something, you are in tune with yourself and you are in tune with the universe— because your center is the center of all. So let this small insight be a climate for you: do only that which you enjoy, otherwise stop.

WHEN BIRTH AND DEATH BECOME ONE

An ancient tree, just by the side of my house, has been dancing in the rain, and its old leaves are falling with such grace and such beauty. Not only is the tree dancing in the rain and the wind, the old leaves leaving the tree are also dancing; there is celebration.

Except man, in the whole existence nobody suffers from old age; in fact, existence knows nothing about old age. It knows about ripening; it knows about maturing. It knows that there is a time to dance, to live as intensely and as totally as possible, and there is a time to rest.

Those old leaves of the almond tree by the side of my house are not dying; they are simply going to rest, melting and merging into the same earth from which they have arisen. There is no sadness, no mourning, but an immense peace in falling to rest into eternity. Perhaps another day, another time they may be back again, in some other form, on some other tree. They will dance again; they will sing again; they will rejoice the moment.

Existence knows only a circular change from birth to death, from death to birth, and it is an eternal process. Every birth implies death and every death implies birth. Every birth is preceded by a death and every death is succeeded by a birth. Hence existence is not afraid. There is no fear anywhere except in the mind of man.

Man seems to be the only sick species in the whole cosmos. Where is this sickness? It should really have been otherwise . . . man should have enjoyed more, loved more, lived more each moment. Whether it is of childhood or of youth or of old age, whether it is of birth or of death, it does not matter at all. You are transcendental to all these small episodes.

Thousands of births have happened to you, and thousands of deaths. And those who can see clearly can understand it even more deeply, as if it is happening every moment. Something in you dies every moment and something in you is born anew. Life and death are not so separate, not separated by seventy years. Life and death are just like two wings of a bird, simultaneously happening. Neither can life exist without death, nor can death exist without life. Obviously they are not opposites; obviously they are complementaries. They need each other for their existence, they are interdependent. They are part of one cosmic whole.

> Existence knows nothing about old age. It knows about ripening, it knows about maturing. It knows that there is a time to dance, to live as intensely and as totally as possible, and there is a time to rest.

But because man is so unaware, so asleep, he is incapable of seeing a simple and obvious fact. Just a little awareness, not much, and you can see you are changing every moment. And change means something is dying—something is being reborn. Then birth and death become one; then childhood and its innocence become one with old age and its innocence.

There is a difference, yet there is no opposition. The child's innocence is really poor, because it is almost synonymous with ignorance. The old man, ripe in age, who has passed through all the experiences of darkness and light, of love and hate, of joy and misery, who has been matured through life in different situations, has come to a point where he is no more a participant in any experience. Misery comes . . . he watches. Happiness comes and he watches. He has become a watcher on the hill. Everything passes down in the dark valleys, but he remains on the sunlit peak of the mountain, simply watching in utter silence.

> ⮞
>
> Just a little awareness, not much, and you can see you are changing every moment. And change means something is dying—something is being reborn. Then birth and death become one, then childhood and its innocence become one with old age and its innocence.

The innocence of old age is rich. It is rich from experience; it is rich from failures, from successes; it is rich from right actions, from wrong actions; it is rich from all the failures, from all the successes; it is rich multidimensionally. Its innocence cannot be synonymous with ignorance. Its innocence can be synonymous only with wisdom.

Both are innocent, the child and the old man. But their innocences have a qualitative difference. The child is innocent because he has not entered yet into the dark night of the soul; the old man is innocent—he has come out of the tunnel. One is entering into the tunnel, the other is getting out of the tunnel. One is going to suffer much; one has already suffered enough. One cannot avoid the hell that is ahead of him; the other has left the hell behind him.

Knowingly or unknowingly, there is a trembling in the heart of every human being: you are becoming old, and after old age the deluge—after old age, death. And for centuries you have been made so much afraid of death that the very idea has become deep-rooted in your unconscious; it has gone deep in your blood, in your bones, in your marrow. The very word frightens you—not that you know what death is, but just because of thousands of years of conditioning that death is the end of your life, you are afraid.

I want you to be absolutely aware that death is not the end. In existence, nothing begins and nothing ends. Just look all around . . . the evening is not the end nor is the morning the beginning. The morning is moving toward the evening and the evening is moving toward the morning. Everything is simply moving into different forms.

There is no beginning and there is no end.

Why should it be otherwise with man? Man is not an exception. In this idea of being exceptional, in being more special than the other animals and the trees and the birds, man has created his own hell, his paranoia. The idea that we are exceptional beings has created a rift between you and existence. That rift causes all your fears and your misery, causes unnecessary anguish and angst in you. And all your so-called leaders, whether religious or political or social, have emphasized the rift; they have widened it. There has not been a single effort to bridge the rift, to bring man back to the earth, to bring man back with the animals and with the birds and with the trees, and to declare an absolute unity with existence.

That is the truth of our being—once it is understood you are neither worried about old age nor worried about death, because looking around you, you can be absolutely satisfied that nothing ever begins, it has been always there; nothing ever ends, it will remain always there.

But the idea of being old fills you with great anxiety. It means now your days of life, of love, of rejoicings are over, that now you will exist only in name. It will not be a rejoicing but only a dragging toward the grave. Obviously you cannot enjoy the idea that you are just a burden in existence, just standing in a queue that is moving every moment toward the graveyard. It is one of the greatest failures of all cultures and all civilizations in the world that they have not been able to provide a meaningful life, a creative existence for their old; that they have not been able to provide a subtle beauty and grace, not only to old age but to death itself.

> Just look all around...the evening is not the end nor is the morning the beginning. The morning is moving toward the evening and the evening is moving toward the morning. Everything is simply moving into different forms.

And the problem becomes more complicated because the more you are afraid of death, the more you will be afraid of life too. Each moment lived, death comes closer. . . . A man who is afraid of death cannot be in love with life, because it is life finally that takes you to the doors of death. How can you love life? It was for this reason that all the religions started renouncing life: renounce life because that is the only way to renounce death. If you don't live life, if you are already finished with the job of living, loving, dancing, singing, then naturally you need not be afraid of death; you have died already.

We have called these dead people saints; we have worshiped them. We have worshiped them because we knew we would also like to be like them, although we don't have that much courage. At least we can worship and show our intentions: "If we had courage or one day if we gather courage, we would also like to live like you: utterly dead." The saint cannot die because he has already died. He has renounced all the pleasures, all the joys; all that life offers he has rejected. He has returned the ticket to existence, saying, "I am no more part of the show." He has closed his eyes.

It happened once that a so-called saint was visiting me. I took him into the garden—there were so many beautiful dahlias, and I showed him those beautiful flowers in the morning sun. He looked very strangely at me, a little annoyed, irritated, and he could not resist the temptation to condemn me, saying, "I thought you were a religious person . . . and you are still enjoying the beauty of the flowers?" On one point he is right, that if you are enjoying the beauty of the flowers you cannot avoid enjoying the beauty of human beings. You cannot avoid enjoying the beauty of women; you cannot avoid enjoying the beauty of music and dance. If you are interested in the beauty of the flowers, you have shown that you are still interested in life, that you cannot yet renounce love. If you are aware of beauty, how can you avoid love?

Beauty provokes love; love imparts beauty.

I said, "On this point you are right, but on the second point you are wrong. Who ever told you that I am a religious person? I am not yet dead! To be religious the basic requirement is to be dead. If you are alive you can only be a hypocrite, you cannot be really religious."

When you see a bird on the wing, it is impossible not to rejoice in its freedom. And when you see the sunset with all the colors spread on the horizon—even if you close your eyes, your very effort of closing the eyes will show your interest. You have been overwhelmed by the beauty of it.

Life is another name of love, and love is nothing but being sensitive to beauty.

I said to that so-called saint, "I can renounce religion but I cannot renounce life, because life has been given to me by existence itself. And religion is just man-made, manufactured by the priests and the politicians—manufactured to deprive man of his joy, to deprive man of his dignity, to deprive man of his humanity itself."

I am not a religious person in that sense. I have a totally different definition of being religious. To me the religious person is one who is totally alive, intensely alive, aflame with love, aware of tremendous beauty all around, and has the courage to rejoice each moment of life and death together. Only a man who is so capable of rejoicing in life and death—his song continues. It does not matter whether life is happening or death is happening, his song is not disturbed, his dance does not waver.

Only such an adventurous soul, only such a pilgrim of existence is religious. But in the name of religion man has been given poor substitutes, false, phony, meaningless, just toys to play with. Worshiping statues, chanting man-made mantras, paying tributes to those who have been cowards and escapists and who were not able to live life because they were so afraid of death, and calling them saints, religion has distracted man from true and authentic religiousness.

You need not be worried about old age. And it is even more beautiful when people start thinking about you as ancient. That means you have attained to the real transcendence, you have lived everything, now it is your maturity. You have not renounced anything but you have simply passed through every experience. You have grown so experienced that now you need not repeat those experiences again and again. This is transcendence.

You should rejoice, and I would like the whole world to understand the rejoicing that is our birthright in accepting with deep gratitude the old age and the final consummation of old age into death. If you are not graceful about it, if you cannot laugh at it—if you cannot disappear into the eternal, leaving a laughter behind—you have not lived rightly. You have been dominated and directed by wrong people. They may have been your prophets, your messiahs, your saviors; they may have been your incarnations of gods, but they have all been criminals in the sense that they have deprived you of life and they have filled your hearts with fear.

> To me the religious person is one who is totally alive, intensely alive, aflame with love, aware of tremendous beauty all around, and has the courage to rejoice each moment of life and death together. Only a man who is so capable of rejoicing in life and death—his song continues.

My effort here is to fill your heart with laughter. Your every fiber of being should love to dance in every situation whether it is day or night, whether you are down or up. Irrespective of the situation, an undercurrent of cheerfulness should continue. That is authentic religiousness to me.

A few sutras for you:

"An ancient man is one who wears his glasses in bed so he can get a better look at the girls he dreams about."

"An ancient man is one who only flirts with young girls at parties so his wife will take him home."

"The beauty of being ancient is that since you are too old to set a bad example, you can start giving good advice."

"Women like the simple things in life—for example, the old men." Once the women start liking you, it means you are finished! They are no longer afraid of you, you are perfectly acceptable.

"Inside every older person there is a younger person wondering what happened."

DROPPING OUT OF THE GAME

You become mature only when meditation has started; otherwise you remain childish. Your toys may go on changing—small children are playing with small toys, and big children, aged children, elderly children are playing with big toys—but there is no qualitative difference.

You can see . . . sometimes your child will do it. He will stand on the table when you are sitting at the side on the chair, and he will say, "Look, Daddy, I am bigger than you." He is standing higher, on the table, and he says, "Look, I am bigger than you," and you laugh at him. But what are you doing? When you have more money, just watch how you walk. You are saying to all the neighbors, "Look! I am bigger than you." Or when you become a president of a country, or a prime minister, look how you walk, with what haughtiness, with what ego. You are telling everybody, "I have defeated you all. I am sitting on the biggest chair." These are the same games! From your childhood to your old age, you go on playing the same games. You can play the game of Monopoly, or you can go and play the real game of monopoly in the stock market—it makes no difference, it is the same game just played on a bigger scale.

Once you understand it, that this is the root of your childishness, the outgoing mind . . . Small children start reaching for the moon, and even the biggest scientists are trying to reach the moon—they have reached. There is not much difference.

Reaching outside, you may reach other stars but you will remain childish. Even if you reach the moon, what are you going to do there? You will be the same! With the same rubbish in your head, with all the holy cow dung that you go on carrying in your heart, you will be standing on the moon. There will be no difference at all! You can be a poor man, you can be very rich; you can be absolutely anonymous, you can be world famous—it makes no difference at all. Unless the mind takes a turn and starts moving inward, unless mind takes a totally new dimension and becomes meditation . . .

Meditation is mind turning toward its own source.

Meditation makes you mature; meditation makes you really a grown-up. Growing in age is not really becoming a grown-up, because I see people eighty years old and still playing games, ugly games of power politics—even at the age of eighty-two, eighty-three, eighty-four! The sleep seems to be so deep. When are they going to awaken? When will they think of the inner world?

And death will take all that you have accumulated—your

> *Mind is a way to understand the object, meditation is a way to understand the subject. Mind is a concern with the contents, and meditation is a concern with the container—the consciousness. Mind becomes obsessed with the clouds and meditation searches for the sky. Clouds come and go, the sky remains, abides.*

power, your money, your prestige. Nothing will be left, not even a trace. Your whole life will be nullified. Death will come and destroy all that you have made; death will come and prove that all your palaces were nothing but palaces made of playing cards.

Maturity is to know something in you that is deathless, to know something in you that will transcend death—that is meditation. Mind knows the world; meditation knows God. Mind is a way to understand the object; meditation is a way to understand the subject. Mind is a concern with the contents, and meditation is a concern with the container, the consciousness. Mind becomes obsessed with the clouds, and meditation searches for the sky. Clouds come and go; sky remains, abides.

Search for the inner sky. And if you have found it, then you will never die. The body will die, the mind will die, but you will never die. And to know it is to know life. What you call life is not real life because it is going to die. Only a meditator knows what life is because he has reached the very source of eternity.

146

PUZZLES

≈

JUSTIFIABLE HOMICIDE

I am fifty, but I don't yet feel really mature and fully grown up. What is the matter with me?

Maybe you have not yet killed anybody. That's a must—if you want to become mature, you have to become a very very skillful murderer. Unless you kill a few persons you will never become mature. You have to kill your parents, you have to kill your teachers, you have to kill your leaders. They are all clamoring inside you, and they don't allow you to become a grown-up person—they go on keeping you childish. They make you a dependent, they don't allow you independence.

It happened: a monk was taking leave from Buddha—he was going far away to spread Buddha's message. When he came to touch his feet, Buddha blessed him and said to his other disciples, "Do you see this blessed monk? He has killed his mother, he has killed his father, he has killed his relatives, he has killed his king." The people were very much surprised, they could not believe their ears: "What is Buddha saying?"

One disciple gathered courage and asked, "Sir, what do you mean? Do you mean a murderer has some virtue? You are calling him blessed?" Buddha laughed and he said, "Not only that, he has even murdered himself—he has committed suicide." Then Buddha sings a song, says a *gatha,* in which he explains what he means by it.

Everybody is brought up as a child. That is your first way into the world; that's how you have been trained for years, to remain a child. Everything was ordered and you were expected to obey. You have become very dependent—you always go on looking for father figures, you always go on looking for authorities to tell you what should be done, what should not be done.

Maturity means the understanding to decide for oneself, the understanding to be decisive on your own. To stand on your own feet—that's what maturity is. But it rarely happens because parents spoil almost every child, more or less. And then there is the school and the college and the university—they are all ready to spoil you. It is very rare that somebody becomes mature.

The society is not happy with mature people. Mature people are dangerous people because a mature person lives according to his own being. He goes on doing his own thing—he does not bother about what people say, what their opinion is. He does not hanker for respectability, for prestige; he does not bother about honor. He lives his own life—he lives it at any cost. He is ready to sacrifice everything, but he is never ready to sacrifice his freedom. Society is afraid of these people; society wants everybody to remain childish. Everybody should be kept at an age somewhere between seven and fourteen—and that's where people are.

In the First World War, for the first time psychologists became aware of this strange phenomenon. For the first time on a large scale, in the army, people's mental ages were researched. And it was a strange discovery: the people in the army had an average mental age of twelve. Your body may be fifty, your mind remains somewhere below fourteen.

Before fourteen you are repressed—because after fourteen repression becomes difficult. By the time a child is fourteen, if he has not been repressed then there is no possibility to repress him ever—because once he becomes a sexual being he becomes powerful. Before fourteen he is weak, soft, feminine. Before fourteen you can put anything into his mind—he is suggestible, you can hypnotize him. You can tell him everything that you want and he will listen to it, he will believe in it.

After fourteen logic arises, doubt arises. After fourteen sexuality arises; with sexuality he becomes independent. Now he himself is able to become a father, now she herself is able to become a mother. So nature, biology, makes a person independent from the parents at the age of fourteen. This has been known long before psychologists entered into the world. Priests have found it out long before—for thousands of years they have watched and they have come to know: If you want to repress a child, if you want to make a child dependent, do it as early as possible—the earlier, the better. If it can be done before seven, success is far more certain. If it cannot be done before fourteen, then there is no possibility to do it.

That's why all kinds of people are interested in children and their education. All the religions are interested, they say children should receive religious education. Why? Before they become independent, their minds should be conditioned.

So the greatest work for a man who really wants to become free, who really wants to become conscious, who really wants to become dehypnotized—who wants to have no limitations of any kind, who wants to flow in a total existence—is that he needs to drop many things from the inside. And when I say, or when Buddha says you have to kill your mother and father, that doesn't mean that you have to go and actually kill your father and mother—but the father and mother that you are carrying within you, the idea.

Watch, observe, and you will find it. You are going to do something and suddenly you will hear your mother's voice: "Don't do it!" You can watch and you will hear the voice, the actual voice—it is a tape inside you. You are going to eat too much ice cream—watch. Suddenly a moment comes when the mother speaks from within: "Don't eat too much—enough is enough. Stop!" And at that time you start feeling guilty.

If you are going to make love to a woman or to a man, suddenly all the teachers are standing there in a queue and saying, "You are going to commit a crime, you are going to commit sin. Beware! This is the trap. Escape before it is too late." Even while you are making love to your wife, your mother and your father, your teachers are there in between, destroying it.

It is very rare to find a man or a woman who really goes totally into love—you cannot go, because for many years you have been taught love is something wrong. How can you drop it suddenly? Unless you are very capable of murdering all these voices . . . great courage is needed. You have to be ready to drop all parental voices, ready to drop all authorities, ready to go into the unknown without any map, on your own. Ready to risk.

It happened that one man, Alexander Eliot, was studying under a Zen Master. For months he was doing meditations, zazen, and he was entering into the deeper waters of his own being. One night he had a dream, a very strange dream. Zen people know about this dream—but for Eliot it was strange; he was a westerner, he was shocked. He relates his dream. . . .

"I recently had a dream in which Bodhidharma appeared. He was a floating huddle of a man—round, ghostly, with bulging eyes and bulbous brow."

Just like me, Bodhidharma is a dangerous man. And Zen people have painted his face, very lovingly, in a very dangerous way. He was not like that—not actually, not physically. Physically he was one of the most beautiful men ever—but if you come across a picture of a Bodhidharma you will start getting scared! If you look into the eyes of Bodhidharma, he looks like a murderer, he is going to kill you. But that's all a Master does. Even in the dream, Alexander Eliot became very much scared and started trembling.

"Was he grinning, or grimacing? His coarse bristling whiskers made this impossible to tell. 'You seem to be a grown-up man,' he whispered through the beard, 'yet you have never killed anyone. How come?'"

Eliot was so shocked that he awoke, and he found himself perspiring and trembling. "What does this strange man mean: How come you have not yet killed anybody?"

That's what I mean when I say if you are feeling you are not yet a grown-up man, it simply shows you have not killed anybody yet. Fifty years is already too late—now don't waste time anymore. Kill immediately all the impressions inside you. Wash your inside of all old tapes, unwind your mind.

Start living your life, from this moment, as if you don't know, as if nobody has taught you anything—fresh, clean, from ABC—and you will see maturity coming very soon. And without maturity life is not worth anything, because all that is beautiful happens only in a mature mind, all that is great happens only in a mature mind. To be a grown-up is a blessing. But people simply grow old, they never become grown-ups. In age they go on growing but in consciousness they go on shrinking. Their consciousness remains in the fetus; it has not come out of the womb, it is not yet born. Only your body is born—you are yet unborn.

> Start living your life, from this moment, as if you don't know, as if nobody has taught you anything—fresh, clean, from ABC— and you will see maturity coming very soon.

Take your life into your own hands—it is *your* life. You are not here to fulfill anybody else's expectations. Don't live your mother's life and don't live your father's life, live your life.

LIFE WITHOUT ATTITUDE

One day you emphasize being mature, another day you say "Be like a child." If I adopt a mature attitude, I feel my child is repressed and starved for expression. If I let my child dance, sing, then childish attitudes come up. What to do?

Being mature does not mean adopting a mature attitude. In fact, adopting a mature attitude will be one of the greatest barriers to becoming mature. Adoption means something imposed, adoption means something cultivated, practiced. It is not arising out of you. It is a mask, a painted face; it is not your real being.

152

That's what everybody has been doing. That's why on the earth people only appear to be mature—they are not, they are utterly immature—deep down, they have adopted attitudes and they remain childish. Their maturity is only skin-deep, or not even that much.

Scratch any man a little bit and you will find childishness arising out of him. And not only the so-called ordinary people—scratch your saints and you will find immaturity arising, or scratch your politicians and your leaders. Go and just watch any parliament of the world and you will never see such a gathering of so many immature and childish people together.

Man has been deceiving himself and others. If you adopt, you will be false, pseudo. I have not been telling you to adopt anything. Be! Adoption is a barrier to being. And the only way to be is to start from the very beginning. Because your parents have not allowed you in your childhood, you are stuck somewhere. The mental age of the so-called normal people is not more than between ten and thirteen years, not even fourteen! And you may be seventy or eighty, but your mental age remains stuck somewhere before you became sexually mature. The moment a person becomes sexually mature, at thirteen or fourteen, he is sealed forever. Then he goes on becoming false and more false. One falsity has to be protected by other falsities, one lie has to be defended by other lies, and then there is no end to it. You become just a heap of rubbish—that's what personality is. Personality has to be dropped, only then does individuality arise. They don't mean the same thing. Personality is just a showcase thing; it is exhibition, it is not reality.

Individuality is your reality, it is not a showplace thing. One can dig as deeply as one wants into you and he will find the same taste. Buddha is reported to have said, "You can taste me from anywhere and you will find the same taste, just as you taste the ocean from anywhere and you will find it salty." Individuality is one whole, it is organic. Personality is schizophrenic: the center is one thing and the circumference is something else, and they never meet. Not only do they never meet, not only are they different, they are diametrically opposed to each other, they are in a constant fight.

> ❧
>
> Individuality is one whole, it is organic. Personality is schizophrenic: the center is one thing and the circumference is something else, and they never meet. Not only do they never meet, not only are they different, they are diametrically opposed to each other, they are in a constant fight.

So the first thing to understand is, never adopt a mature attitude. Either be mature or be immature. If you are immature, then be immature—by being immature you will be allowing growth. Then let the immaturity be there; don't be false, don't be insincere about it. If you are childish, so you are childish—so what? Be childish. Accept it, go with it. Don't create a division in your being, otherwise you are creating a fundamental madness. You just be yourself.

Nothing is wrong with being childish. Because you have been taught that something is wrong in being childish you have started adopting attitudes. From your very childhood you have been trying to be mature, and how can a child be mature? A child is a child; he has to be childish.

But it is not allowed, so small children become diplomats—they start pretending, they start behaving in false ways, they become lies from their very beginnings and the lie goes on growing. And then one day you start searching for truth; then you have to go into the scriptures, and scriptures contain no truth at all. The truth is contained in your being, that is the real scripture. The Veda, the Koran, the Bible—they are in your consciousness! You are carrying all that is needed by you, it is a gift from God. Everybody is born with truth in his being—life is truth. But you started learning lies.

Drop all lies. Be courageous—and of course you will feel a great fear arising in you, because whenever you drop the personality, your childishness, which has never been allowed, will surface. And you will feel afraid: "What! Am I going to be childish at this point? When everybody knows that I am a great professor—or a doctor or an engineer—and I have a PhD and I am going to be childish?" The fear arises—the fear of public opinion, of what people will think.

> Let immaturity be there, don't be false, don't be insincere about it. If you are childish, so you are childish—so what? Be childish. Accept it, go with it. Don't create a division in your being, otherwise you are creating a fundamental madness. You just be yourself.

That same fear has destroyed you from the very beginning. The same fear has been the poison: "What will my mother think? What will my father think? What will people think, the teachers and the society?" And the small child starts becoming cunning—he will not show his heart. He knows that will not be accepted by others, so he creates a face, a camouflage. He will show that which people want to see. This is diplomacy, this is being political—this is poison!

Everybody is political. You smile because it pays to smile, you cry because it is expected of you to cry. You say a certain thing because that makes things easy. You say to your wife, "I love you," because that keeps her quiet. You say to your husband, "I will die without you, you are the only person in my world, you are my life," because he expects you to say it, not because you are feeling it. If you are feeling it then it has beauty, then it is a real rose. If you are simply pretending, massaging his male ego, buttressing him because you have some ends to fulfill through him, then it is an artificial flower, a plastic flower.

And you are burdened with so much plastic—that is the problem. The world is not the problem. The so-called religious people go on saying, "Renounce the world." I say to you that the world is not the problem at all. Renounce the falsity—*that* is the problem. Renounce the artificial—*that* is the problem. There is no need to renounce your family but renounce all that pseudofamily that you have created there. Be true, authentic. Sometimes it will be very painful to be true and to be authentic, it is not cheap. To be untrue and inauthentic is cheap, convenient, comfortable. It is a trick, a strategy to protect yourself; it is an armor. But then you will miss the truth that you have been carrying in your soul. Then you will never know what God is, because God can be known only within you. First within, then without; first in, then out—because that is the closest thing to you, your own being. If you miss God there how can you see God in Krishna, Christ, Buddha? All nonsense. You cannot see God in Christ if you cannot see God in yourself. And how can you see a God in yourself if you are continuously creating lies around yourself? The lies are so much that you have almost forgotten the way to your being. You are lost in the jungle of lies.

Friedrich Nietzsche has said that man cannot live without lies; and for about ninety-nine percent of people he is right. Why cannot man live without lies? Because lies function as buffers, shock absorbers. Lies function like a lubrication; you don't go on colliding with people. You smile and the other smiles—this is lubrication. You may be feeling angry inside, you may be full of rage, but you go on saying to your wife, "I love you." To express the rage is to get into trouble.

But remember, unless you can express your rage you will never know how to express your love. A man who cannot be angry cannot be loving either, because he has to repress his anger so much that he becomes incapable of expressing anything else—because all things are joined together inside your being, they are not separate. There are no watertight compartments between anger and love; they are all together, mixed with each other. It is the same energy. If you repress anger you will have to repress love too. If you express love, you will be surprised—anger is arising with it. Either suppress all, or all will have

> To be untrue and inauthentic is cheap, convenient, comfortable. It is a trick, a strategy to protect yourself, it is an armor. But then you will miss the truth that you have been carrying in your soul.

to be expressed. You have to understand this arithmetic of your inner organic unity. Either be expressive or be repressive. The choice is not that you can repress anger and express love; then your love will be false because it won't have any heat, it won't have the quality of warmth. It will just be a mannerism, a mild phenomenon, and you will always be afraid in moving deeper into it.

People only pretend to love because they are expected to love. They love their children, they love their wife or husband, their spouses, their friends, because they are expected to do certain things. They fulfill these things as if they are duties. There is no celebration in them. You come home and you pat your child's head just because that is expected, just because that is the thing to do, but there is no joy in it—it is cold, it is dead. And the child will never be able to forgive you, because a cold pat on the head is ugly. And the child feels embarrassed, you feel embarrassed.

You make love to your woman but you never go far into it. It can take you really far out, it can take you to the ultimate bliss, you can dissolve into it. But if you have never allowed your anger and you have never been dissolved in your anger, how can you allow love to dissolve you? And it has happened many times—you will be surprised—that a lover has killed the woman because he allowed his love and then suddenly the anger came. It is a well-known fact that many times a lover has simply killed the woman, suffocated her—and he was not a murderer; the society is responsible. He simply dared too much and went too deeply into love. When you go too deep you become wild, because your civilization is on the surface. Then anger arises, then all that is hidden inside you arises and then you are almost mad.

To avoid that madness you make love in a very superficial way.

It is never a tremendous phenomenon. Yes, people are right when they say that it is just like a sneeze: it relaxes tensions, it relieves you of a certain energy that was getting heavy on you. But this is not the real picture of love. Love has to be ecstasy—not like a sneeze, not just a release but a realization, a liberation. Unless you know love as a liberation, as ecstasy, as samadhi, you have not known love. But that is possible only if you are not pseudo, if you have been authentic in everything—if you have allowed anger, if you have allowed laughter, if you have allowed tears, if you have allowed all. If you have never been a preventive force, you have never been holding anything, you have never been controlling—if you have lived a life of uncontrol. And remember, by uncontrol I do not mean a life of licentiousness. The life of uncontrol can be of great discipline, but the discipline is not imposed from the out- side. It is not an adopted attitude. The discipline comes from your own inner experiences. It comes from the encounter with all the possibilities of your being. It comes by experiencing all the aspects, it comes by exploring all the dimensions. It comes out of under- standing. You have been in anger and you have understood some- thing in it—that understanding brings discipline. It is not control. Control is ugly, discipline is beautiful.

The word *discipline* basically means capacity to learn, hence the word *disciple*. It does not mean control, it means to be capable of learning. A disciplined man is one who goes on learning through life experiences, who goes into everything, unafraid—who risks, who explores and adventures, who is always ready to go into the dark night of the unknown, who does not cling to the known and who is always ready to commit mistakes, who is always ready to fall in a ditch and who is always ready to be laughed at by others.

Only people who are courageous enough to be called fools are able to live and love and know and be.

Maturity comes through more and more, deeper and deeper experiences of life, not by avoiding life. By avoiding life you remain childish.

One thing more: when I say be like a child I don't mean be childish. A child has to be childish; otherwise he will miss that great experience of childhood. But whether you are young or old, childishness simply shows that you have not been growing. To be like a child is a totally different phenomenon. What does it mean? One, the child is always total—whatsoever the child is doing he becomes absorbed in it, he is never partial. If he is collecting seashells on the beach, then all else simply disappears from his consciousness, then all that concerns him are the seashells and the beach. He is absorbed in it, utterly lost in it. That quality of being total is one of the fundamentals of being like a child. That is concentration, that is intensity, that is wholeness.

> A disciplined man is one who goes on learning through life experiences, who goes into everything, unafraid—who risks, who explores and adventures, who is always ready to go into the dark night of the unknown.

And the second thing: a child is innocent. He functions from a state of not knowing. He never functions out of knowledge because he has none. You always function out of knowledge. Knowledge means the past, knowledge means the old and the told, knowledge means that which you have gathered. And every new situation is new, no knowledge is applicable to it. I'm not talking about engineering or technology—there, the past is applicable because a machine is a machine. But when you are behaving in a human atmosphere, when you are communicating with alive beings, no situation is a repetition of any other. Each situation is unique. If you want to function rightly in it you will have to function through a state of ignorance, like a child. Don't bring your knowledge into it, forget all knowledge. Respond to the new as new, don't respond to the new from the old. If you respond from the old you will miss: there will be no bridge between you and what is happening around you. You will always be late, you will always go on missing the train.

People go on dreaming again and again of a train, and they always miss it. In the dream, the person is rushing and running and reaches the station, and by the time he reaches, the train has left. This dream happens again and again to millions of people, this is one of the commonest dreams. Why does this dream come again and again to millions of people on the earth? They are missing life. They are always late. There is always a gap. They try, but the bridge is never made. They cannot commune, they cannot get into anything, something hinders. What is it? It is knowledge that hinders.

I teach you ignorance. And when I say be like a child I mean always keep learning, never become knowledgeable. Knowledge is a dead phenomenon, learning is an alive process. And the learner has to remember this—he cannot function from the standpoint of knowledge.

Have you not watched and observed it? Little children learn so fast. If a child lives in a multilingual atmosphere he learns all the languages. He learns the language that the mother speaks, the father speaks, the neighbors speak—he may learn three, four, five languages very easily, with no problem. Once you have learned a language then it becomes very difficult to learn another language because now you start functioning from the standpoint of knowledgeability. It is said you cannot teach the old dog new tricks. It is true. But what makes a dog old? Not physical age, because a Socrates goes on learning to the very end, even while he is dying. A Buddha goes on learning to the very end. What makes a dog old? Knowledge makes a dog old.

> Respond to the new as new, don't respond to the new from the old. If you respond from the old you will miss: there will be no bridge between you and what is happening around you. You will always be late, you will always go on missing the train.

Buddha remains young, Krishna remains young. We have not a single statue of Buddha or Krishna that depicts them as old. Not that they never became old! Krishna lived up to the age of eighty, became very old, but something in him remained always young, childlike. He continued to function from the state of not knowing.

So first, when I say be like a child I mean be total. And the second thing is remain a learner, function from the state of not knowing. That's what innocence is: to function from not knowing is innocence.

And the third thing, and the last: a child has a natural quality of trust; otherwise he cannot survive. When the child is born he trusts the mother, trusts the milk, trusts that the milk will be nourishing him, trusts that everything is okay. His trust is absolute, there is no doubt about anything. He's not afraid of anything. His trust is so much that the mother is afraid—because the child can go and start playing with a snake. His trust is so much that a child can go and poke his hand into the fire. His trust is so much—he knows no fear, he knows no doubting. That is the third quality.

If you can know what trust is, if you can learn again the ways of trust, then only will you know what godliness is, then only will you come to realize what truth is. This has to be understood.

Science depends on doubt—that's why the whole of education has become the education of doubt. Science depends on doubt, it cannot grow without doubt. Religiousness depends on trust, it cannot happen without trust. These are diametrically opposite directions.

Remember, if you bring trust into a scientific work you will miss the whole point. You will not be able to get anything, you will not be able to discover anything. Doubt is the methodology there. You have to doubt and doubt and doubt; you have to go on doubting until you stumble upon something that cannot be doubted, that is indubitable. Then only, in helplessness, you have to accept it—but still with a grain of doubt that tomorrow new facts may arise and the whole thing will have to be dropped. So only for the time being . . . Science never comes to any ultimate truth but only tentative truth, approximate truth. Only for the time being is it accepted as truth because who knows?—tomorrow researchers will find new facts, new data. So science comes only to hypotheses, tentative, arbitrary. What Newton had discovered has been thrown down the drain by Albert Einstein, and what he has discovered will be thrown out by somebody else. In science, doubt is the methodology. Trust is not needed. You have to trust only when there is no possibility to doubt—and that too only tentatively, for the time being, in a kind of helplessness. What can you do? Because no further doubt is possible. You have looked from all sides and all doubts are dissolved and a kind of certainty has arisen.

Religion is a diametrically opposite dimension. Just as in science doubt is the method, in religion trust is the method. What does trust mean? It means that we are not separate from existence, that we are part of it, that this is our home. That we belong to it, that it belongs to us, that we are not homeless, that the universe is a mothering universe. We can be children with the universe just as the child trusts that whenever the need arises the mother will come and take care—when he is hungry she will come and feed him, when he feels cold the mother will come and hug him and give warmth, love, care. The child trusts. All that he needs to do whenever he is in some need is scream and cry so that the mother's attention is attracted toward him, that's all. Religion says this universe is our mother or our father, hence these expressions. Jesus called God "Abba," which is far better than father. *Father* is a formal word, *abba* is informal. If you have to translate *abba* rightly, it will be closer to daddy than to father. But to call God *Daddy* looks a little absurd; the church won't allow it. The church will say this is not right. But Jesus used to call him *Abba,* which is daddy.

> Just as in science doubt is the method, in religion trust is the method. What does trust mean? It means that we are not separate from existence, that we are part of it, that this is our home.

In fact, a prayer has to be informal. "Father" looks so far away. It is no wonder that by calling God the Father we have put him far away, distant somewhere, in heaven. Daddy feels closer—you can touch him, he is almost tangible, you can talk to him. With a God-Father sitting somewhere high in the heavens you can go on shouting and still you cannot trust whether you will be able to reach him.

Religion is a childlike approach toward existence: the world becomes a mother or a father. You are not against nature, you are not fighting with nature. There is no fight, there is great cooperation. The fight seems to be stupid and absurd.

Doubt does not work in religious experience, just as trust does not work in scientific exploration. Science means exploring the without and religion means exploring the within. Science is the religion of things, religion is the science of being. Just as you cannot see a flower through the ear—howsoever sensitive an ear you have, howsoever musical an ear you have, you cannot see a flower through the ear. The ear can only catch sounds, it has its limitations. If you want to see the color, the light, the form, you will have to look through the eyes. The eyes are so beautiful but they have their limitations—you cannot hear music through the eyes. Even the greatest music will not be able to penetrate the eyes. The eyes are deaf, you will have to hear through the ears.

Doubt is the door to things. Trust is the door to being. Only through trust is godliness known.

And remember, you can commit the fallacy in two ways. The so-called religious people have been fighting science, the church has been fighting science. That was a foolish fight because the church wanted science to depend on trust. And now science is taking revenge—now science wants religion to also depend on doubt, on skepticism, on logic. Man is so foolish that he goes on repeating the same mistakes again and again. The church in the Middle Ages was stupid; now people who think they are scientists are doing the same stupidity again.

The man of understanding will say that doubt has its own world. You can use doubt as a method, but it has its limitations. And so has trust its own world, but it also has its limitations. There is no need to use trust to know about things and there is no need to doubt about the inner; then you are creating a mess. If trust were used for scientific exploration, science would not have been born at all. That's why in the East science has remained very primitive.

I have come across Indian scientists—even a scientist in India who may have all the education that is possible in the West, who may have won awards, or maybe even if he is a Nobel laureate, remains somewhere, deep down, unscientific, superstitious. He goes on trying in some ways—known or unknown to him, aware or unaware—to impose trust on the outside world. And the very, very religious person from the West remains somewhere, deep down, doubtful. The West has explored the possibilities of doubt and the East has explored the possibilities of trust.

You have to use both. And I call that man a man of understanding who can use both. When working in a scientific lab he uses doubt, skepticism, logic; when praying in his temple, meditating, he uses trust. And he is free—he is neither bound by trust nor bound by doubt.

Don't be bound by your ears or by your eyes, otherwise you will remain poor. You have both! So when you want to see use eyes, and when you want to listen close your eyes. It is not accidental that when listening to music people close their eyes. If you know how to listen to music you will close your eyes, because eyes are no longer needed.

So is it with doubt and trust. Trust is the quality of the child. These three qualities—the quality of being total, the quality of remaining ignorant in spite of knowledge, and the quality of trust—this is the meaning.

Childishness is a kind of sentimental emotional state. That is not needed for you. Every child has to be allowed to be childish, as every adult has to be allowed to be adultish, but an adult can also have the qualities of being a child. Childishness is not needed, that tantrum quality is not needed, that sentimentality is not needed—but maturity can cope perfectly well with the qualities of being like a child. There is no contradiction between them. In fact, you can become mature only if you are like a child.

But if your childishness has remained unfulfilled, you have to allow it. Let it come, and let it be fulfilled—the sooner the better, otherwise it will go on clinging to you to your very end. Allow it expression and it will be gone. Once it is allowed

> Every child has to be allowed to be childish, as every adult has to be allowed to be adultish, but an adult can also have the qualities of being a child. Childishness is not needed, that tantrum quality is not needed, that sentimentality is not needed—but maturity can cope perfectly well with the qualities of being like a child.

it will have its time and will go, and it will leave you very much fulfilled. It is better to go into it right now than postpone it— because the more you postpone the more difficult it becomes— and then you will find a childlike quality arising. Childishness will disappear. It will be temporarily there, then it will be gone and your child will be fresh and young. And after that child is attained you will start growing. Then you can become mature. You cannot mature with all the lies that you are carrying around yourself. You can mature only when you become truthful, when you become true.

FROM SEX TO SENSUALITY

Is it really possible to drop sex by going through it? It seems my mind and body will never stop asking for it.

But why are you in such a hurry to drop it? If you are in such a hurry to drop it, you will never be able to drop it. The very hurry, the very desire to drop it will not allow you to understand it totally. How can you understand something that you have already decided is wrong, that it has to be dropped? You have already judged, you have not listened! Give a chance to your sexuality.

I have heard that Mulla Nasruddin was made a justice of the peace. The first case came into court and he heard one party. Then he said, "Wait, now listen to my judgment." The court clerk was puzzled because he had not yet heard the opposite party.

He leaned close to Nasruddin and said, "What are you doing, sir? Judgment? You have not heard the other side!"

Nasruddin said, "What do you mean, the other side? Do you want to confuse me? Now things are clear! And if I hear the other side I am going to be confused. Then judgment will be very difficult."

But will it be a judgment? You have not heard the other party at all. You have heard your so-called saints down the ages—they are very vocal. Their whole sex energy has become their articulateness against sex—you have heard them. You have never given a chance to your own sexuality to have its say. No, this will not be right, you are prejudiced. Why? Who knows? It may not be the thing to be dropped. Then . . . ? Who knows? It may be the right thing to go on carrying it. Remain open. I'm not saying anything except remain open. Meditate deeply. While you are making love, let meditativeness penetrate your love act. Watch! And forget all the prejudices that you have been brought up with—all those conditionings against sex make you more sexual, and then you think sexuality is a problem for you. It is not sex energy itself that is the problem. It is the antisexual mind that creates perversion.

All the religions have been sources of perversion. When I say all the religions, I don't mean Buddha, I don't mean Mahavir, I don't mean Krishna, I don't mean Christ or Mohammed; I mean the followers. They have been the source, a great source. And what happened really? They watched Buddha and they saw that sex had disappeared, so they made it a dictum that sex has to disappear. You can become a Buddha only when sex disappears—they made a dictum, they made it a rule. And this is just putting things in a wrong order. Sex disappears because Buddha has come to his inner source, not the other way round. Not that he has dropped sex and that's why he has become a Buddha—he has become a Buddha, hence sex has disappeared. But from the outside people watched Buddha and they saw sex had disappeared—so drop sex if you want to become a Buddha. Buddha is not interested in money, so they thought, "Become disinterested in money if you want to become a Buddha."

But these are all wrong approaches! This is not looking for the cause, but misunderstanding the effect as the cause. The cause is inside buddhahood. He has become awakened to his inner being. When one becomes awakened to one's inner being one is so blissful that who bothers about sex? Who begs for small moments of pleasure from somebody else? Who goes begging? When you are the emperor and you have the treasure, the infinite treasure within yourself, you will not go to ask a woman, you will not go to ask a man, to give you a few moments of pleasure. And you know that she is begging and you are begging—both are beggars standing before each other with their begging bowls: "You give me a few moments of pleasure, I will give you a few moments of pleasure." And both are beggars! How can beggars give?

But I'm not saying something is wrong in it. While buddhahood has not yet happened to you, all things will continue—nothing is wrong. For the moment don't judge—*judgment* is wrong. Just become more watchful, more accepting, more relaxed with your energies. Otherwise you will be in the trouble Christian saints have been in down the ages.

I have heard about Jerome, a very famous Christian saint. He was so much against the body that he used to whip his body every day. Blood would flow from his body, and thousands of people would come to see this great austerity. Now both are ill: Jerome is a masochist and the people who gather together to see this great phenomenon are sadists. They want to torture people, they have a great desire to torture—they cannot, and this man is doing it on his own; they are very happy watching it. Both are pathological.

Jerome condemned the body as the "vile body," the "sack of excrement." He was tormented in his cave by visions of beautiful girls. He permitted marriage but very grudgingly—because it was the only way of producing virgins. The reason is to produce virgins, the most perfect beings on the earth. So sex is a necessary evil, that's why he permitted marriage; otherwise it is a sin.

Another man, Clement of Alexandria, wrote: "Every woman should be overwhelmed with shame at the thought that she is a woman—because she is the door to hell."

I have always been surprised by these people. If woman is the door to hell, then no woman can enter hell—the door cannot enter itself. Man can enter through the woman into hell, okay—and what about woman? They must be all in heaven, naturally! And what about man? If woman is the door to hell, then what about man? Because these scriptures have been written by men and all these saints were men.

> While buddhahood has not yet happened to you, all things will continue—nothing is wrong. For the moment, don't judge—*judgment* is wrong. Just become more watchful, more accepting, more relaxed with your energies.

In fact, women have never been so neurotic; that's why you don't hear of many women saints. They have been more normal, they have been more down-to-earth. They have not been so foolish as man has proved to be. They are more graceful and more round in their being, more rooted in the earth, more centered. Hence, you don't hear about many women like Clement of Alexandria—you cannot find a parallel woman. No woman has ever said that man is the door to hell.

And it is not that women have never been mystics. No, there was Meera, and there was Rabiya, and there was Lalla in Kashmir—but they have never said anything like this. On the contrary, Meera said that love is the door to God.

And another saint, Origen, castrated himself—murderers, suicidal people! All this repression created great pathology in the Christian world. One nun, Mathilde of Magdeburg, felt God's hand fondling her bosom. Now why give God such trouble? But if you avoid men, then you will start creating fantasies. Then you will have to put too much into your fantasies. Christine Ebner, another nun, believed herself pregnant with a child by Jesus. There were monks who dreamed of copulating with the Virgin Mary. And because of great repression, the convents and monasteries became the visiting places of the so-called evil spirits. These demons took the form either of succubi, beautiful girls who jumped into the beds of would-be male saints, or incubi, handsome young men who interrupted the sleep or the meditations of the nuns. Such pathology arose in Christianity that people started dreaming all kinds of things. And many nuns confessed in the courts that the devil came in the night and made love to them. They even described the devil's physiology, what kind of sexual organ he has—forked, so that it enters both the holes.

Pathology, ill people, gone neurotic! And those nuns confessed in the courts that once you have made love to the devil then no man can ever satisfy you—he is the greatest lover, he brings such orgasms. This nonsense happened not only in Christianity, it happened all over the world. But Christianity comes to the utmost peak in it.

Please, don't be against sex; otherwise you will fall into the trap of sex more and more. If you want to get rid of it you will never get rid of it. Yes, there is a point of transcendence when sex disappears—but it is not that you are against it. It disappears only when you find better blessings arising inside your being, never before that. The higher has to be found first, then the lower disappears of its own accord.

Let it be a fundamental rule in your life: never be against the lower—search for the higher. *Never* be against the lower, search for the higher, and the moment the higher dawns on you suddenly you will see that the interest in the lower has disappeared.

You ask, "Is it possible, really possible, to drop sex by going through it?"

I'm not saying that. I'm saying that if you go through it you will be able to understand it. Understanding is freedom, understanding liberates.

I'm not against sex, so don't be in a hurry to drop it. If you want to drop it, how can you understand it? And if you don't understand it, it will never disappear! And when it disappears, it is not that sex is simply cut off from your being, it is not that you become a nonsexual being. When sex disappears, in fact you become more sensuous than ever because the whole energy is absorbed by your being.

A Buddha is more sensuous than you are. When he smells, he smells more intensely than you smell. When he touches, he touches more totally than you touch. When he looks at the flowers, he sees the flowers more beautiful than you can see—because his whole

⤚

Please, don't be against sex, otherwise you will fall into the trap of sex more and more. If you want to get rid of it you will never get rid of it. Yes, there is a point of transcendence when sex disappears—but it is not that you are against it. It disappears only when you find better blessings arising inside your being, never before that.

sexual energy has spread all over his senses. It is no longer localized in the genitals, it has gone all over the body. Hence, Buddha is so beautiful. The grace—the unearthly grace—from where is it coming? It is sex—transformed, transfigured. It is the same mud that you were decrying and condemning which has become a lotus flower.

So never be against sex; it is going to become your lotus flower. And when sex is really transfigured, then you understand what a great gift sex was from God to you. It is your whole life, it is your whole energy. On the lower planes, on the higher planes—it is the only energy you have. So don't carry any antagonism, otherwise you will become repressive. A man who represses cannot understand. And a man who cannot understand is never transfigured, never transformed.

AN ONGOING JOURNEY

Your consciousness is far bigger than the whole universe. It is infinitely infinite. You cannot come to a point where you can say, "Enough." There is always more and more. There is always a possibility to go on growing. And growing, maturing is such a beautiful experience, that who wants to stop it?

We are stopped in every way. Even a great scientist like Albert Einstein has used only fifteen percent of his intelligence. What to say about ordinary people? They never use more than five percent.

Just think, if Einstein was capable of using one hundred percent of his intelligence he would have given the world unimaginable richness.

And if everybody is using his consciousness one hundred percent, then who would like to go to heaven and live with those dead saints, dodos, masochists, whose only qualification was self-torture?—which is simply a psychological disease.

If everybody uses one hundred percent intelligence, we can create paradise here. There is no need to go anywhere. We can give man as long a life as he wants, as healthy a life as he wants. We can create so much wealth that it becomes just like air—nobody needs to hoard it.

Using your intelligence totally means the beginning of maturity.

Awareness is only a methodology. First, become aware of how

much intelligence you are using, or are you using it at all? Belief and faith are not intelligent. They are taking a decision against your intelligence. Awareness is a methodology to watch how much intelligence you are using. And just in that watching you will see that you are not using much. There are many ways awareness will make you alert. You can use it.

Awareness will bring you to your one hundred percent intelligence, will make you almost divine. And awareness does not stop there. Awareness helps you to use your intelligence fully.

Intelligence is your outgoing road, connecting you to the world, to the objects. Intelligence will give you more science, more technology. In fact, there is no need for man to work anymore, if we can use our intelligence. Machines can do almost everything. And you need not go on carrying, according to Jesus, the cross on your shoulders. That is stupid.

Machines can do everything, and you are freed for the first time from slavery; otherwise, it is only in name that you feel you are free. But you have to earn the bread, you have to earn some money to make

> *If everybody uses one hundred percent intelligence, we can create paradise here. There is no need to go anywhere. We can give man as long a life as he wants, as healthy a life as he wants. We can create so much wealth that it becomes just like air—nobody needs to hoard it. Using your intelligence totally means the beginning of maturity.*

a shelter, a house, money for medicine, money for other things.

So it seems you are independent, but you are not. The old slavery is no more there; now you are not chained, but there are invisible chains—your children, your old parents, your sick wife, your job.

Man is not yet free. He is working eight hours and still carrying files home. Working late in the night at home, working on Sundays. Still the files go on growing on his table, and there seems to be no end to it. Enter any office and you will see these people, see these people's tables. Can you call them free? Just think about yourself: Are you really free?

There is only one possibility, supertechnology, which can do all the work and man will be completely free to be creative. You can play your guitar, sing your song. You can paint, you can make sculptures. You can do thousands of things to beautify this earth. You can make beautiful gardens, ponds.

There is so much to be done to make this earth beautiful. If there is a God, even he may start feeling jealous, thinking that it was wrong to drive Adam and Eve out of heaven; those people are doing far better. And it will be no surprise that if there is a God, one day he will knock on your doors and say, "May I come in?"

Awareness will release your intelligence, will make you mature. And then maturity goes on growing.

Ordinarily you simply grow old, you don't grow up. Growing old is one thing, growing up is totally different. All animals grow old: no animal, except man, can grow up. Growing old simply means you are coming closer to your death, not much of an achievement. Growing up means you are coming to realize the deathless, the eternal that has no beginning and no end. All fear disappears. All paranoia disappears. You are not mortals.

Growing old, you are mortals. Growing up, you become immortals. You know you will be changing many houses. You will be changing many forms, but each form will be better than the past one, because you are growing, you are maturing. You deserve better forms, better bodies. And, finally, there comes a moment when you don't need any body. You can remain just pure consciousness spread all over existence. It is not a loss, it is a gain.

> ☙
>
> There is so much to be done to make this earth beautiful. If there is a God even he may start feeling jealous, thinking that it was wrong to drive Adam and Eve out of heaven; those people are doing far better. If there is a God, one day he will knock on your doors and will say, "May I come in?"

A dewdrop slipping from the lotus leaf into the ocean. . . . You can think the poor drop is lost, has lost its identity. But just look from a different dimension: the drop has become the ocean. He has not lost anything, he has become vast. He has become oceanic.

Awareness is the method to first wake up your intelligence, then to wake up your being, then to help you become mature, give you the realization of immortality, and ultimately to make you one with the whole.

MATURATION IS AN ONGOING PROCESS. There is no full stop, not even a semicolon anywhere . . . it goes on and on. The universe is infinite. So is the possibility of your maturing.

You can become so huge. . . . Your consciousness is not confined to your body. It can spread all over existence and all the stars can be within you. And there is no place where you will find a plate that says, "Here ends the universe." It is just not possible. It never begins; it never ends.

And you are part of it. You have been here always and you will be here always. Only forms change, and forms don't matter. What matters is the content. So remember that, particularly in America, where containers matter more than the content. Who cares about the content? The container has to be beautiful.

Remember, the container is not you. You are the content. Forms change, your being remains the same. And it goes on growing, maturing, goes on becoming more enriched.

And you ask, "What is the relationship between awareness and maturity?"

Awareness is the method; maturation is the result. Become more aware and you will have more maturity; hence, I teach you awareness and don't talk about maturity. It is going to happen if you are aware.

There are three steps of awareness.

First, become aware of your body—walking, chopping wood, or carrying water from the well. Be watchful, be alert, aware, conscious. Don't go on doing things like a zombie, like a somnambulist, a sleepwalker.

When you have become aware of your body and its actions, then move deeper—to your mind and its activity, thoughts, imagination, projections. When you have become deeply aware of the mind, you will be surprised.

When you become aware of your bodily processes, you will

be surprised there too. I can move my hand mechanically, I can move it with full awareness. When I move it with full awareness, there is grace, there is beauty.

> *Remember, the container is not you. You are the content. Forms change, your being remains the same. And it goes on growing, maturing, goes on becoming more enriched.*

I can speak without awareness. There are orators, speakers. . . . I don't know any oratory; I have never learned the art of speaking, because to me it looks foolish. If I have something to say, that is enough. But I am speaking to you with full awareness, each word, each pause . . . I am not an orator, not a speaker.

But when you are aware of speaking, it starts becoming art. It takes on the nuances of poetry and music. This is bound to happen if you speak with awareness. Then every gesture, every word has a beauty of its own. There is grace.

When you become aware of the mind, you are in for a greater surprise. The more you become aware, the less thoughts move on the track. If you have one hundred percent thoughts, there is no awareness. If you have one percent awareness, there are only ninety-nine percent thoughts, in exact proportion. When you have ninety-nine percent awareness, there is only one percent thought, because it is the same energy.

As you become more aware, there is no energy available for thoughts; they die out. When you are one hundred percent aware, the mind becomes absolutely silent. That is the time to move still deeper.

The third step: to become aware of feelings, moods, emotions. In other words, first the body—its action; second, the mind—its activity; third, the heart and its functions.

When you move to the heart and bring your awareness there, again a new surprise. All that is good grows, and all that is bad starts disappearing. Love grows, hate disappears. Compassion grows, anger disappears. Sharing grows, greed disappears.

When your awareness of the heart is complete, the last surprise and the greatest surprise: you don't have to take any step. A quantum leap happens on its own accord. From the heart, you suddenly find yourself in your being, at the very center.

There you are aware only of awareness, conscious only of consciousness. There is nothing else to be aware of, or to be conscious of. And this is the ultimate purity. This is what I call enlightenment.

> Awareness is the method, maturation is the result. Become more aware and you will have more maturity, hence, I teach you awareness and don't talk about maturity. It is going to happen if you are aware.

And this is your birthright! If you miss, only you are responsible. You cannot dump the responsibility on anybody else.

And it is so simple and natural, that you just have to begin.

Only the first step is difficult. The whole journey is simple. There is a saying that the first step is almost the whole journey.

About the Author

O sho is a contemporary mystic whose life and teachings
have influenced millions of people of all ages and from
all walks of life. He has been described by the *Sunday
Times* in London as one of the "1000 Makers of the 20th Century"
and by *Sunday Mid-Day* (India) as one of the ten people—along
with Gandhi, Nehru, and Buddha—who have changed the destiny
of India.

About his own work Osho has said that he is helping to create
the conditions for the birth of a new kind of human being. He has
often characterized this new human being as "Zorba the Buddha"—
capable of enjoying both the earthy pleasures of a Zorba the Greek
and the silent serenity of a Gautama the Buddha. Running like a
thread through all aspects of Osho's work is a vision that encom-
passes both the timeless wisdom of the East and the highest potential
of Western science and technology.

He is also known for his revolutionary contribution to the science of inner transformation, with an approach to meditation that
acknowledges the accelerated pace of contemporary life. His unique
"Active Meditations" are designed to first release the accumulated
stresses of body and mind, so that it is easier to experience the
thought-free and relaxed state of meditation.

Meditation Resort

❧

Osho Commune International

O sho Commune International, the meditation resort that
Osho established in India as an oasis where his teachings
could be put into practice, continues to attract thousands
of visitors per year from more than one hundred different countries
around the world. Located about one hundred miles southeast of
Bombay in Pune, India, the facilities cover thirty-two acres in a
tree-lined suburb known as Koregaon Park. Although the resort
itself does not provide accommodation for guests, there is a plentiful
variety of nearby hotels.

The resort meditation programs are based on Osho's vision of
a qualitatively new kind of human being who is able both to par-
ticipate joyously in everyday life and to relax into silence. Most
programs take place in modern, air-conditioned facilities and in-
clude everything from short to extended meditation courses, creative arts, holistic health treatments, personal growth, and the "Zen"
approach to sports and recreation. Programs are offered throughout
the year, alongside a full daily schedule of Osho's active meditations.

Outdoor cafes and restaurants within the resort grounds serve
both traditional Indian fare and a variety of international dishes, all

made with organically grown vegetables from the commune's own farm. The campus has its own private supply of safe, filtered water.

For booking information call (323) 563-6075 in the USA or check osho.com for the Pune Information Center nearest you.

For more information: www.osho.com

A comprehensive Web site in different languages, featuring an on-line tour of the meditation resort, information about books and tapes, Osho information centers worldwide, and selections from Osho's talks.

Osho International
570 Lexington Avenue
New York, NY 10022
Telephone: (212) 588-9888
Fax: (212) 588-1977
email: osho-int@osho.org.